The Impact of Climate Change on Sundarbans:

Implications for India-Bangladesh Relations

The Impact of Climate Change on Sundarbans:

Implications for India-Bangladesh Relations

PRASHANT KUMAR SHARMA

ADROIT

Adroit Publishers

NEW DELHI • KATHMANDU

ISBN : 978-81-87393-59-7

2018

Published by
ADROIT PUBLISHERS 4675/21, Ganpati Bhawan, Ansari Road,
Daryaganj, New Delhi-110 002 Phone : 011-23266030
adroitpublishers@gmail.com
C/O Vajra books, Thamel, Jyatha,
Kathmandu, Nepal l KTM: +977-9808357451

Typeset in Garamond Premier Pro by Arun, Akriti Graphic Solution, Delhi-110081 E-mail: arun263923@gmail.com, Ph: 9999414390

Dedicated to

My Maa & Pitaji
Smt. Suraj Moni Devi & Shri Ram Pravesh Sharma

Contents

Acknowledgement

The present study is an updated version of my dissertation, submitted to the School of International Studies, Jawaharlal Nehru University, New Delhi, for the award of the Degree of Master of Philosophy.

I express my profound sense of gratitude to my revered teacher and competent supervisor Prof. Mahendra P Lama for giving me inspirations to undertake this study. I extend my thanks to him for providing me creative, constructive and substantial ideas throughout my period of research. Most importantly, this work could not have been formulated in a profound and thematic structure, nor could I reach to this stage had I not received his innovative and thought provoking comments and criticism.

I am thankful to Prof. Sanjay K Bhardwaj, for his ceaselessly valuable suggestions and constant showering of his love and support to me throughout my period of research. I am also thankful to Prof. Sugata Hazra, Director, School of Oceanographic Studies, Jadavpur University, Kolkata, whose valuable works have been useful in writing this dissertation. My thanks also go to Prof. Jayanta Bandyopadhyay, for his invaluable suggestions. My thanks also go to Prof. Sanjay Paswan, for his moral support. I am grateful to Prof. Savita Pande, Prof. P Sahadevan, Prof. Amita Batra, Prof. Rajesh S. Kharat, and others at the Centre for South Asian Studies, for constantly providing me with their moral and intellectual support throughout my period of research.

I would like to extend my appreciation to all the staff members of the libraries of Jawaharlal Nehru University and South Asia Foundation, New Delhi, for their excellent cooperation in providing me all the required materials and help. My appreciation is due to the Centre for Science and Environment, New Delhi, and World Wide Fund For Nature (WWF-India), as their reports on the Sundarbans helped me get substantial inputs for this study.

Moreover, I am highly grateful to my inspirational teacher, Prof. Santanu Sengupta, Head of Department, Political Science at Seth Anandram Jaipuria College, University of Calcutta, for giving me his special academic attention and made me feel special throughout my graduation days. My thanks also go to Prof. Gautam Ray, for extending his all-round invaluable cooperation and help both to me and my family in Kolkata.

I express my gratitude to my college teachers – Dr. Bhaswati Roy, Mr. Sidhartha Dutta Gupta, Ms. Monalisa Mohanta, Ms. Shyamashree Roy, Mrs. Swagata Bhattacharya, and Dr. Soma Bhattacharya and all others at Department of Political Science, Seth Anandram Jaipuria College, University of Calcutta, for helping to prepare grounds in Political Studies. I am also grateful to my teachers –Prof. Aneek Chatterjee, Prof. Nandalal Chakraborty, Prof. Abdus Samad Gayen, Prof. Pradip Basu, Prof. Prasanta Roy, Prof. Bikash Chandra Dutta, Prof. Gautam Kumar Basu, Dr. Zaad Mohammad, and Dr. Satyabrat Sinha and all others at the Department of Political Science, Presidency University, Kolkata, for bestowing upon me their never-ending moral support, love, and good wishes. I also convey my sincere thanks to my NCC teacher, Mr. Abhijit Das, at Seth Anandram Jaipuria College, for always inspiring, encouraging and inculcating in me a strong sense of leadership during my graduate days.

I have been indebted to some of my teachers – Shri Ramdhari Kewat, Shri Siyaram Yadav, Shri Satyananda Rai, Shri Deo Nath Singh,

Shri Ram Lakhan Pandit, Shri Shailendra Kumar Rai, Shri Kailash Ji Aggrawal who have contributed in a mammoth way to mould me at the early stage of my school life. I reached to this stage of higher learning simply because of them. I am greatly obliged to them.

I must acknowledge the friendly atmosphere provided to me by my friends Jigme Wangdi, Pawan, Praveen Kodabagi and Satya Prakash while undertaking this study. My heartfelt thanks also go to some of my senior friends Dr. Azizur Rahman Azami, Dr. Sarada Prasanna Das, Dr. Vinay Kumar, Dr. Amar Singh, Dr. Ram Pratap, Mr. Subhajit Naskar, Mr. Sudipta Bhaarat, Mr. Joy Deep Saha, Md. Raza Abbas Haidri, and Mr. Dharamraj Kumar, for their inspiration and cooperation.

Furthermore, I convey my heartiest regard to some of my well-wishers, Md. Alimuddin and Mr. Mannuel (dear friends of my father) for sincerely providing me all rounds of support at the outset of my M.Phil days while I was in Kolkata. I extend my sincere gratitude also to my friends – Mr. Philip Abraham and Mr. Jogendra Kumar Prasad, for their constant support to me during my stay at Kolkata.

I would be at a loss if I do not extend my special and sincere thanks to my dear friend, Mr. Nandan Saha, a Research Scholar at Presidency University, and Mr. Shubham Singh, University of Bristol, United Kingdom, for providing me painstakingly moral and financial support throughout my period of research.

Finally, I sincerely thank my friend Ms. Adrita Dutta Roy for her support in editing this work. A special recognition is due to M/s Adroit Publishers, New Delhi, for publishing this work with utmost zeal and promptness.

I am greatly indebted to my *Bhaiya* – Mr. Sushant Kumar Sharma, and my younger sisters- Lakshmi Sharma and Puja Sharma, for the care and affection they have expressed towards me.

Prashant Kumar Sharma

List of Table

List of Map

List of Figure

List of Abbreviations

ADB	Asian Development Bank
AGW	Anthropogenic Global Warming
BNP	Bangladesh Nationalist Party
BIISS	Bangladesh Institute of International and Strategic Studies
BCCSAP	Bangladesh Climate Change Strategy and Action Plan
BSF	Border Security Force
BGL	Below Ground Level
CSE	Center for Science and Environment
CBD	Convention on Biological Diversity
CCC	Climate Change Cell
DFID	Department for International Development
DGmodel	Dynamic Game models
ECA	Ecologically Critical Area
GLOF	Glacial Lake Outburst Floods
GOB	Government of Bangladesh
ISD	Indian Sundarbans Delta
IMD	Indian Meteorological Department
IPCC	Intergovernmental Panel on Climate Change
IDP	Internally Displaced Person
IEA	International Environmental Agreement
IUCN	International Union for Conservation of Nature
LDCF	Least Developed Countries Fund
LECZ	Low Elevation Coastal Zone

LSAT	Land Surface Air Temperature
MOU	Memorandum of Understanding
MPEDA	Marine Product Export Development Authority
NAPCC	National Action Plan on Climate Change
NAPA	Adaptation Program on Action
NFAP	National Forestry Action Programme
NEP	National Environment Policy
NEAMA	National Environment Assessment and Monitoring Authority
NGT	National Green Tribunal Act
NTPC	National Thermal Power Corporation
OECD	Organization of Economic Cooperation and Development
PPT	Part per Thousand
PSMSL	Permanent Service for Mean Sea Level
RSG	Reduced Stage Game models
RCP	Representative Concentration Pathway
SAPCC	State Action Plan on Climate Change
SAARC	South Asian Association for Regional Cooperation
SMRC	SAARC Meteorological Research Centre
SARS	Severe Acute Respiratory Syndrome
SST	Sea Surface Temperatures
SEDP	Socio-economic Development Programme
SAD	Sundarbans Affairs Department
SDB	Sundarbans Development Board
SRF	Sundarban Reserve Forest
UNSC	United Nations Security Council
UNEP	United Nations Environment Programme
UNDP	United Nations Development Programme
UNESCO	United Nations Educational, Scientific and Cultural Organization
UNFCCC	United Nations Framework Convention on Climate Change
WII	Wildlife Institute of India
WMO	World Meteorological Organization
WTI	Wildlife Trust of India
WWF	World Wildlife Fund for Nature

Chapter One

Introduction

The climate of the earth is incessantly changing over time. Many scientific studies have corroborated these changing phenomena. Nevertheless, what exactly caused the advent of climate change is widely debated at both the scientific and the political fore. The Intergovernmental Panel on Climate Change (IPCC) has attributed this phenomenon of global warming induced climate change largely to the anthropogenic activities. Every nook and corner of the globe is experiencing the irrevocable impact of climate change. Some parts of the world, especially low-lying coastal regions have been the most adversely affected by this phenomenon. India and Bangladesh have been identified among the 27 countries most vulnerable to the climate change induced accelerated sea level rise. The Sundarbans is massively affected by the impact[1] of climate change, which is the world's largest mangrove ecosystem and the single block of tidal halophytic mangrove forest. It is an archipelago of several hundreds of islands, which is crisscrossed by a maze of tidal rivers, estuaries and creeks.

1. The term 'impact' has been used primarily to indicate the effects of climate change on natural and human system. Generally, Impacts is used to refer the effects on lives, livelihoods, health status, ecosystems, economic, social, and cultural assets, services (including environmental), and infrastructure owing to the interaction of climate changes or hazardous climate events that occur within a specific time period and the vulnerability of an exposed society or system. Moreover, Impacts are referred to as consequences and outcomes. The climate change impact on geophysical systems, encompassing floods, droughts, and rises in sea-level, are a subset of impacts, which is called physical impacts (IPCC AR5 2014).

The most important indicator of climate change is the accelerated increase in global temperatures. Changes in global temperatures have set in motion a number of forces that are causing rises in global sea levels, melting of glaciers, ice sheets and snow covers, and glacial lake outbursts that consequently lead to flooding, reducing supplies of water for drinking, farming, industry and other similar kind of outcome. These outcomes have serious environmental and human security implications.[2] Most of the recent scientific assessment of global climate change shows that rise in sea level will have a significant impact on coastal environment and their biotic communities, as well as human settlements. Smith (2009) stated, "Climate change is taking place and will cause sea level to rise for centuries even if greenhouse gas emissions are stabilized."[3] IPCC in its Third Assessment Report (2001) projected that sea level will rise approximately one meter in the twenty first century. The Fourth Assessment Report (2007) predicted sea level rises up to 0.6 meters or more by 2100.

The Sundarbans is situated in the vast delta of Bay of Bengal shaped by the convergence of the Ganges, Brahmaputra and Meghna rivers across southern part of India and Bangladesh. Extending through India to Bangladesh, it covers an area of about 26,000 square km that forms the largest single stretch of mangrove vegetation of which 60% of mangrove forest area located in Bangladesh and the remaining 40% rests with India. The Bangladeshi part of Sundarbans accounts for 4.2% of country's total land area and holds 40% of the Bangladesh's total forest tracts.

---

2. Alley et al. (2007), "Summary for Policy makers", Contribution of working Group I to the "Climate Change 2007, The Physical Science Basis", IPCC, Geneva. Quoted in Smith, Anthony Oliver (2009), "Sea Level Rise and the Vulnerability of Coastal Peoples: Responding to the Local Challenges of Global Climate Change in the 21st Century", ***United Nations University-UNU-EHS-Institute for Environment and Human Security***, No.7/2009:17.

3. Smith, Anthony Oliver (2009), "Sea Level Rise and the Vulnerability of Coastal Peoples: Responding to the Local Challenges of Global Climate Change in the 21st Century", ***United Nations University-UNU-EHS-Institute for Environment and Human Security***, No.7/2009:17.

It stretches over the districts of 24 Parganas of West Bengal, Khulna, Backergunge and Sathkhira of Bangladesh. The administrative boundary of the Indian part of Sundarbans is spread over two districts of West Bengal i.e. South 24 Parganas and North 24 Parganas. The Sundarbans falls at a close south to the tropic of cancer. The Indian Sundarbans exists between the latitude 21°32' to 22°40'N and longitude 88°03' to 89°E. The Bangladeshi part of Sundarbans lies between the latitude 21°30' to 22°30' N and longitude 89°12' to 90°18'E.

The boundaries of the Indian Sundarbans extend over the area from the river Hooghly in the west to the Ichamati-Raimangal (Herobhanga or Harinbari River) in the east, and Dampier-Hodges line drawn in 1829-1830 in the north to the Bay of Bengal in the south. The Bangladeshi Sundarbans consists of three wildlife sanctuaries: Sundarbans West, East and South. This is bounded in north by Bagerhat, Khulna and Sathkhira districts, in south by Bay of Bengal, in the east by Baleswar (or Haringhata) river, Perojpur and Barisal districts, and in the west by Raimangal and Harinbhaga rivers, which partially form the boundary with India.

In the Indian Sundarbans, out of 108 islands, 54 are inhabited and the population is around 4.4 million whereas Bangladeshi Sundarbans consists of about 200 islands with a population spread of around 7.5 million. Indian part of the Sundarbans consists of 19 Community Development (CD) Blocks, and these blocks come under the two districts of North 24-Parganas and South 24-Parganas.

The Zila Parishad is the highest form of local self-government at the level of district followed by the Panchayat Samiti at the level of Block. Moreover, the Gram Panchayat functions at the cluster of village level. The civil administration is a corresponding institution to this kind of Panchayat administration. The civil servants head the civil administration; and this administration of the state ceases at the block level. The departments that exert the broadest influence administratively over the delta of Indian Sundarbans are the Sundarbans Affairs Department (SAD) and the Forest Department. In order to resolve the socio-economic backwardness of this region, the Sundarbans Development Board (SDB) was established in 1973. This department was replaced by the Sundarbans Affairs Department in 1994.

The Indian Sundarbans is declared as a '**Tiger Reserve**' in 1973, a '**National Park**' in 1984, a '**Biosphere Reserve**' by UNESCO in 1989, and a '**World Heritage Site**' by UNESCO in 1987. The three wildlife sanctuaries of Bangladeshi Sundarbans were set up in 1977 under the Bangladesh Wildlife (Preservation) (Amendment) Act, 1974. Given its ecological and socio-economic significance, the Reserve Forest of the Sundarbans was named the '**Ramsar site**' in 1992. The UNESCO owing to its rich ecological resources has declared these three-wildlife sanctuaries as World Heritage Site in 1997. The Bangladeshi portion of the Sundarbans forest has been classified under two Forest Divisions under the Khulna circle for managing, conserving and proper use of the natural resources of the forest. In addition to this, forest management is classified into four administrative ranges that include Satkhira, Khulna, Sarankhola and Chandpai and has 16 forest stations. This region is further divided into 55 compartments and 9 blocks. Moreover an area of 10 km around the Sundarbans reserve forest has been declared as the 'Ecologically Critical Area (ECA)' in 2010 by the Department of Environment, where all developmental activities are prohibited.

It is rather difficult to attribute the present changes in the Sundarbans directly and wholly to climate change. However, the changes in the Sundarbans are highly perceptible in respect of changes in temperature of the sea surface, precipitation pattern, occurrence of extreme weather events, and changes in the sea level. With the decreasing freshwater flow from Himalayan rivers predicted for the dry season (dry season getting drier) and gradual increase in sea level is likely to enhance the severity of salinity ingression in the Sundarbans, which would affect all aspects of the Sundarbans. This has also enhanced the process of coastal erosion jeopardizing the existence of the Sundarbans. Though the process of erosion and accretion have been a natural phenomenon, certain well evident pattern of changes in climate and anthropogenic activities in recent years have added to these natural phenomena aggravating situations in the whole tract of the Sundarbans.

The surface air temperature over the area indicates a rise of 0.019 degree centigrade per year. Cyclones exhibit an increase in intensity with its frequent occurrence. The Indian Sundarbans is currently under the threat of severe coastal erosion because of rises in the relative sea level. The eastern coast of India is more vulnerable to sea level rise than western coast. Nevertheless, the exact reason is not observed in case of the Indian Sundarbans but for the Bangladeshi Sundarbans monsoonal rains and land subsidence have been the dominant factors.

The people of Sundarbans feel exposed to the changes in frequency and magnitude of extreme weather events. Over the last 120 years, 26 percent increase in severe cyclonic events over the Bay of Bengal has been observed escalating in the post monsoon period. The northern part of the Bay of Bengal during the period 2007-2009 has endured four cyclones Sidr, Nargis, Bijli and Aila with powerful winds, heavy rainfall and flooding, leading to the intense coastal erosion and failure of embankments. The cyclone Aila of 2009 was the most dramatic of the climatic disasters to have recently hit the Sundarbans.

Climate change induced sea level rise has two kinds of impact. The first impact is that land is lost to the sea and landholding is drastically decreasing asserting more pressure on the agriculture on ever-smaller landholdings. Moreover, the second impact is that the land lost to the sea is complicated to reclaim for the purpose of cultivation because the salinity devastates the productivity of the soil.

The rising trends of the sea level have jeopardized the future viability of the Sundarbans. The sea level has risen by 3.18 mm in the past decade because the Pacific Ocean is in La Nina Phase. The most of the islands in the Sundarbans are low-lying, and even the mainland does not have any pointed elevation near the seafront thereby any rise in sea level would have a direct impact on the people residing there. It is reported that many islands have lost to sea level rise and some are on the verge of submersion. Sea level rise has caused intrusion of saline water over land rendering the loss of agricultural productivity and contaminating the quality of fresh water. Reduction of freshwater due to salinity intrusion pushes the Tigers upwards often resulting into the man-tiger confrontation. Besides the land loss caused by sea level rise, another factor contributing in land loss is the constant erosion of embankments built to prevent seas from intruding the islands. There exists a constant battle between human and the sea to stop the large measure of land being dragged away.

Mangrove ecosystem has been the lifeline of the Sundarbans' existence as it protects the coast from heavy wind, tidal waves, coastal erosion and seawater intrusion, engenders substantial quantities of fishery resources and makes available many useful forestry products. Since the last few decades, certain natural and man-made problems are posing grave threat to the existence of the entire Sundarbans. These have disturbed the complex food chain and the wild life population, and enhanced coastal erosion, diminished soil fertility. Due to these changes mangrove ecosystem also provides less resistance now to the ravages of gales and storms over the land.

Though massive anthropogenic factors are also responsible for reduction in the forest resources, the impact of climate change has been found to be adding fuel to the fire. The Sundarbans is endowed with a plethora of natural resources, which provides the livelihood opportunities to the inhabitants dependent on it. The forest dependents living around the Sundarbans are mainly engaged in the collection of fish, fuel wood, Golpata, crabs, honey and waxes. The constant decline in the forest cover is posing threat on the livelihood patterns of the people of the Sundarbans. This enhances possibilities of conflict between the resource and livelihood and will be exacerbated further by displacement and livelihood deprivation.

The climate change will have its impact also upon the supporting service of the Sundarbans. A study reveals that with 32 cm SLR by 2050 the area of Sundari trees would reduce by 14% and 45% by 2100; and by 2100 the appropriate area of 'Gewa' would shrink maximum 7% owing to rises in the sea level. Moreover, owing to the climate change impact, the forest dependent diverse wildlife habitat would be highly exposed. Bangladesh would be left to face a decimated fishing industry, large scale flooding and the possible loss of endangered animals. It is stated that the fresh water channels are becoming increasingly saline and possibly a rise in the sea level will definitely push the saline water back up into the channels.

The maritime boundary dispute over the New Moore islands was apparent to have been the bone of contention for many years between India and Bangladesh. The magnitude of the climate change impact could be located in the submergence of New Moore islands. With the permanent submergence of this island the long-standing dispute between India and Bangladesh is put to an end. In this backdrop the issues generated in wake of the climate change have also added a new dimension in the relationship particularly over the issues of the Sundarbans.

There is growing possibilities that climate change impact will cause serious cross-border security threats between India and Bangladesh. It is expected that many millions of Bangladeshi would cross over to India in the future owing to the rises in sea level that might aggravate further the ongoing dispute between India and Bangladesh over the issue of illegal migration. Enormous environmental crisis and the mounting climate change impacts in Bangladesh have triggered cross-border migration to the Indian Sundarbans region. There is a perpetual exodus of migrants from Bangladesh into this region who could be labeled 'crisis migrants' encroaching into the Indian Sundarbans in anticipation of intimidations in their own country.

At this backdrop, this work studies the likely impact of climate change on Sundarbans in its entirety, which examines issues like loss of mangrove forest, salinity intrusion, coastal erosion, tidal inundation, livelihood conditions, socio-cultural ramification, cross border security, displacement and illegal migration and refugee movement. This also assesses how these critical issues will impinge upon India-Bangladesh relation. The climate change could cause immense human insecurity that both countries need to address. More seriously, a situation of this nature has never occurred particularly in the context of geography-community-natural resources neutral character, and nature and impact of climate change. The intensive and extensive bilateral relations between India and Bangladesh are going to be affected in a variety of new ways and means.

Bangladesh retains 57 cross-boundary rivers of which 54 are shared with India. Any loss in the quality and quantity of shared water upstream in India would definitely affect the parts of Bangladesh. It is stated that ecosystems do not recognize the territorial boundary. Any damage in one part of the Sundarbans is bound to affect the other part. Therefore, it also triggers an opportunity for both countries to cooperate and coordinate on the matter of common concern.

India and Bangladesh are however, taking initiative to safeguard the euphonious diversity and existence of Sundarbans. Jairam Ramesh, former Environment and Forest Minister, Govt. of India, proposed the establishment of a joint forum between India and Bangladesh to protect the rich diversity of the Sundarbans ecosystem. It is decided that two sides viz. India and Bangladesh, would work on conducting a joint census of tigers in the tract of Sundarbans. The sixty percent of these tigers remain on the Bangladeshi side of the Sundarbans. The area of cooperation between these countries is adaptation to climate change. In the last 20 years, five islands are reported to have been inundated. Sugata Hazara states that climate change can affect everyone beyond the geographical boundaries. These events have added a new dimension to the relationship in the realm of cooperation.

The second chapter deals with the theoretical underpinnings of climate change. In the domain of social science, the most debated theories like non-traditional and non-military security, Game theory, Non-Cooperative theory of emission cap determination, Geopolitical theory, and the like have been discussed in relation to the phenomenon of climate change. This chapter also discusses the changing nature, contents, dimensions and implications of climate change.

The third chapter is categorized into two sections. First an ecological profile is drawn which deals with geography, physiography, ecosystem, environment and biodiversity of the Sundarbans. After this a socio-economic profile is explored in which focus is laid on history and cultural values, demography, social structure and political economy of the Sundarbans.

The fourth chapter broadly examines and assesses the assumed and likely impacts of climate change on various aspects of the Sundarbans.

The fifth chapter attempts to understand the emerging complexities and various dimensions of climate change in the Sundarbans and their implications for India-Bangladesh relation. India has been wary in the backdrop of the changing phenomena. Some of the critical issues that is dealt in this chapter relates to displacement among the inhabitants and likely creation of refugees and internally displaced people and their crossing the borders, the spillage of the oil and cross border environmental injuries and the conflicts in the Sundarbans that may lead to instabilities on both sides of the border and issues related to bio-piracy, natural resource exploitations, natural and manmade disasters, etc.

Finally, in the concluding chapter the major findings of the entire chapters are highlighted.

Both available primary and secondary data has been used for the analysis of climate change impact on the Sundarbans and its implications for India-Bangladesh relation. This study is based on qualitative research method. The primary data includes documents and reports released by both Governments of India and Bangladesh through their respective ministries pertaining to environment and climate issues, and reports and documents published by NGOs and INGOs. The secondary data is based on available existing literature such as books, academic journals, newspaper reports, and internet material.

Chapter Two

Climate Change: Theoretical Underpinnings

In the domain of social science the most debated theories like non-traditional and non-military security[4], Game theory[5], Non-Cooperative theory of emission cap determination[6], Geopolitical theory[7], all have been discussed in relation to the phenomenon of climate change. A question however remains whether the phenomenon of climate change is new. What are the changing nature, contents, dimensions and implications of climate change and how real is its directions in terms of its reach and impact. Moreover, what India and Bangladesh have done at the legal and policy level to sort out the outstanding issues of climate change?

"*Climate change* indicates to a change in the state of the climate that can be identified by changes in the mean and/or the variability

4. "Traditional and Non-traditional Security," ***Institute for Security & Development Policy***, [Online: web] Accessed 12 July 2015 URL: http://www.isdp.eu/issues/traditional-and-non-traditional-security.html.

5. Finus, Michael (2002), "Game Theory and International Environmental Cooperation: Any Practical Application?" in Christoph Bohringer, Michael Finus and Carsten Vogt (eds.) ***Controlling Global Warming***, Cheltenham, UK: Edward Elgar Publishing Limited.

6. Shah, Sudhir A. (2004), "A Noncooperative Theory of Emissions –Cap Determination", in Michael A. Toman, Ujjayant Chakraborty, Shreekant Gupta (eds.) ***India and Global Climate Change: Perspective from a developing Country***, India: Oxford University Press.

7. Halden, Peter (2007), "The Geopolitics of Climate change: Challenges to the International System", ***FOI, Swedish Defence Research Agency***, Stockholm, Sweden.

of its properties and that persists for an extended period, typically decades or longer. Climate change may occur owing to the natural internal processes or external forces such as modulations of the solar cycles, volcanic eruptions, and continual anthropogenic changes in atmosphere's composition or in land use. In addition to this, Framework Convention on Climate Change (UNFCCC), in its Article 1, elucidates climate change as "a change of climate that is directly or indirectly triggered by human activity which alters the composition of the global atmosphere and which is in addition to natural climate variability observed over comparable time periods." Therefore, the UNFCCC distinguishes between climate change caused by human activities changing the composition of the atmosphere, and climate variability due to natural causes."[8]

It is believed by several climatologists that earth's temperature fluctuates slowly over time. Various theories have evolved regarding the climate change and global warming. In 1824, the first theory of global warming became known at a time when Jean Baptiste Joseph Fourier, a French mathematician, exposed that temperature of the earth was slowly increasing.[9] He argued that solar radiation is trapped by the earth's atmosphere that is again reflected back towards the earth.

The climate change issue is a significant part of the global discourse today. However, there is a visible dearth of unanimity over the question of inception of the phenomenon of climate change. However, these issues became part of the scientific discourse since 1896 when Svante Arrhenius, a Swedish chemist, analyzed the linkages between atmospheric carbon dioxide and air temperature in order to clarify the

8. IPCC (2014), "Summary for policymakers", in Field, C.B. (eds.) ***Climate Change 2014: Impacts, Adaptation, and Vulnerability. Part A: Global and Sectoral Aspects. Contribution of Working Group II to the Fifth Assessment Report of the Intergovernmental Panel on Climate Change,*** Cambridge: Cambridge University Press, p.5.

9. [Online: web] URL:http://www.globalwarmingarchive.com/History.aspx.

existence of the ice ages.[10] Svante's analysis of the atmosphere made him forecast that if carbon dioxide in the atmosphere doubled, the earth's mean average annual temperature would be warmer by varied degrees. His estimates, nevertheless, fetched little public attention and concern.[11]

Moreover, Etkins and Ho argued that the huge degrees of attention have been paid on the issues of climate change since that time and especially in the past few decades. They stated that sensing the susceptibility to future climate change thrust due to the high concentrations of greenhouse gases that might be detrimental to humankind and natural ecosystems, there have been an extensive commotion on this subject that encompasses scientists, politicians, special interests groups and the general public.[12]On the very outset of this chapter, it has been mentioned that the climate of the earth is incessantly changing over time. From the late 14th century to the end of 19the century the earth went through the 'little ice age.'[13] By that time, severe cold and insensitive conditions led to the number of famines and the expansion of glaciers, particularly in the Alps, Scandinavia, Iceland and Alaska.[14] The scientists were in search of finding an answer, as the temperature of the earth had steeply soared by the 1850s.

Climate change is often linked to the changes in modern climate, which is a result of human activities in recent times. It is strongly believed that human beings have always influenced their environment, and it is only since the inception of the industrial revolution, mid

10. Arrhenius, S. (1896), "On the influence of carbonic acid in the air upon the temperature of the ground", ***Philosophical Magazine***, 41: 237-276; Etkin, David and Elise Ho (2007), "Climate Change: Perceptions and Discourses of Risks", ***Journal of Risk Research***, Vol.10, No.5, p.624

11. Etkin, David and Elise Ho (2007), "Climate Change: Perceptions and Discourses of Risks", ***Journal of Risk Research***, Vol.10, No.5, p.624

12. Ibid.624

13. [Online: web] URL: http://www.globalwarmingarchive.com/History.aspx.

14. Ibid.

18th century that the impacts of man-made activities have begun to traverse globally.[15] R. K. Pachaury has enumerated that the problems of climate change came to the light in 1988 at a time when North America incurred severe drought and an unusually hot summer.[16] These occurrences not only led the experts to make an assessment, but also the global worries for the phenomenon of global warming and climate change resulted in the establishment of the Intergovernmental Panel on Climate Change (IPCC) in 1988 through the efforts of the World Meteorological Organization (WMO) and the United Nations Environment Programme (UNEP).[17]

Nitin Desai[18] in *Climate Change: economic and historical perspective* has clarified that the issues of climate change were not the case very long ago. For him, it meant that the climate change phenomenon is a recent one. Desai believes that atmospheric scientists were the early movers on the concerns of climate change rather than the activists of the green movement.[19] The references to the climate change are embedded in the Brundtland commission's report titled as *Our Common Future,* published in 1987. The green movement could not exert its pressure upon the issues of climate change when this commission report was

15. Chinnamai, A. Mariyappan, and M. Selvaraj (2011), "Mitigating Climate change: the Indian Perspective", ***The Research Journal of Sherubtse College***, pp.11-15.

16. Pachaury, R.K. (2004), "Global Climate Change: Indian Perspective Revisited and Restated", in Michael A. Toman, Ujjayant Chakraborty, and Shreekant Gupta (eds.***) India and Global Climate Change: Perspective on Economic and Policy From a Developing Country,*** India: Oxford University Press. pp. 341-346.

17. Ibid. 341.

18. Nitin Desai was the Deputy Secretary general of the UN Conference on Environment and Development, in 1992

(The Rio Earth Summit), and later he continued as under Security General in charge of Sustainable Development and Policy Coordination at the UN headquarters. He was close to the negotiation process on the Climate convention right up to the time into force in 1997, in both capacities.

19. Desai, Nitin (2010), "Climate Change: economic and historical perspectives", in The Energy and Resources Institute (eds.) ***The Environment Emergency: Exploring solutions for a sustainable future***", New Delhi: TERI Press. pp.118-120.

being made, and not even in the Rio process. At this stage, the focus remained on the issues of classical conservation.

Moreover, Desai stipulated that the first two heads of the state from the developing world highlighted the matter of climate change at the global level – Ershad, the former President of Bangladesh and Gayoom, the former President of Maldives. These heads of state raised the issue in the 1980s. President Gayoom who mentioned climate change for the first time at the United Nations General Assembly, and not any leader from the Organization of Economic Cooperation and Development (OECD) countries. The first intergovernmental organization to set up a process on climate change was not in the UN, but the secretariat of the Commonwealth. This secretariat set up a group under Martin Holgate. Concerns came from most of the developing countries, the scientific community, and certain INGOs outside the UN. The political process that we see today is emanated from those concerns of developing and scientific world. In the early days, people used to use the term 'global warming', which in the views of Desai was misconstrued. In the Northern Hemisphere, folks did not think of this warming of the world as a bad idea. Therefore, the terminology got changed to climate change.[20]

Following the above enumeration on the span of climate change, it is palpable that an enigma of climate change is not new to the scientific world. Rather we can say that these phenomena are new to the political world at a time when its adverse impact was felt socially, economically and politically across the nook and corner of the globe. That is a different thing that whether it had positive or negative effects, however the most important thing as of now is that people are getting awareness of at least the concept of climate change, if not to the full extent. The impact of climate change has potentiality to destabilize countries like Maldives, Bangladesh, India and Kiribati, and particularly the low-

20. Ibid.119

lying countries and islands. Climate change issues have emerged as a core concern in form of non-military and non-traditional security threat respecting no territorial boundary, and requiring no passport to move. With the advent of globalization, after the collapse of the Soviet Union, these issues got pace and attention of the world move away from the traditional form of security.

2.1. Theories of Climate change

Bast[21] has delineated seven theories of climate change – Anthropogenic Global Warming (AGW), Bio-thermostat,[22] Cloud Formation and Albedo,[23] Human Forcings besides Greenhouse Gases,[24] Ocean Currents,[25] Planetary Motion,[26] and Solar Variability.[27]

---

21. Bast, Joseph L. (2010*), "Seven Theories of Climate change",* Chicago: The Heartland Institute.

22. This theory of climate change holds that negative feedbacks from biological and chemical processes entirely or almost entirely counteract whatever positive feedbacks might be caused by rising carbon dioxide. These processes act as a "global bio-thermostat" keeping temperatures in equilibrium (Bast 2010:8).

23. This theory relies largely on observational data reported by the number of researchers which assumes that changes in the formation and albedo of clouds create negative feedbacks that cancel out all or nearly all of the warming effects of higher levels of carbon dioxide (Bast 2010:12).

24. This theory postulates that the greatest influence of humankind on climate is not its greenhouse gas emissions, but its transformation of surface of earth by clearing forests, irrigating deserts, and building cities (Bast 2010:14).

25. This theory of climate change asserts that global temperature variations over the past century-and-a-half, and especially in the past 30 years, were due to the slow-down of the ocean's Thermohaline Circulation (THC). Atmospheric scientist, William "Bill" Gray is the chief proponent of this theory (Bast 2010:17).

26. The Planetary motion theory contends that most or all of the warming of the latter part of the twentieth century can be elucidated by the natural gravitational and magnetic oscillations of the solar system, which is induced by the movement of the planet through space. In addition, these oscillations regulate solar variations and other extra-terrestrial influences of earth that cause climate change (Bast 2010:20).

27.. This theory propounds that solar variability accounts for most or all of the warming in the late twentieth century and will dictate climate in the twenty-first century regardless of man-made greenhouse gas emissions (Bast 2010:23).

However, these theories of climate change and many other models remained confined to the scientific discourse to a large-extent. These add new dimensions to the dominant anthropogenic global warming theory. On the other hand in the climate change discourse, a spectrum of theories that has a strong degree of inter-disciplinary studies has emerged as a part of the social science research. These include theory of non-traditional security threat, Game theory, non-cooperative theory of emission cap determination and geopolitical theory. However, given the prominence of anthropogenic global warming theory it deserves an independent elaboration.

2.1.1. Anthropogenic Global Warming Theory

The theory of climate change that most people are acquainted with is commonly known as anthropogenic (man-made) global warming. This implies that anthropogenic activities leading to greenhouse gases, particularly carbon dioxide, are the preponderate reason of the global warming that transpired in the last 50 years. However, in the last few years, anthropogenic theory of global warming has been overwhelmed by the onset of the new researches that do not claim man-made carbon dioxide as a major cause of climate change.

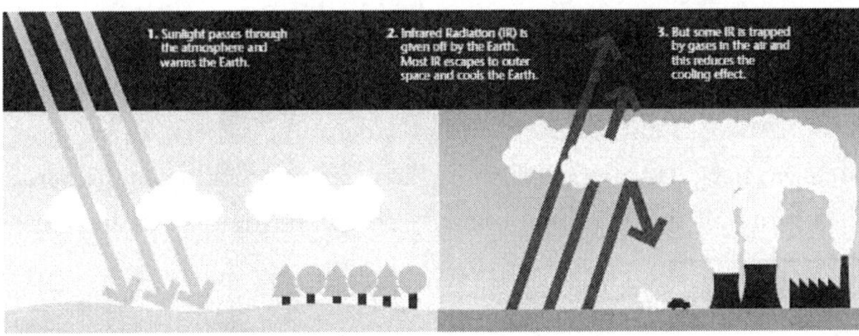

Figure: 2.1. Warming of Atmosphere

Source-URL:http://www.freecriticalthinking.org/climate-change/123-anthropogenic-global-warming-theory.

The UK Met Office believes that climate change has been caused by the man-made greenhouse gases. This change has become alarmingly significant and might be unsustainable in the long- run. The above Figure 2.1 shows how earth is getting heated. In the left side of the Figure, which is yellow, shows the solar rays hitting the earth and consequently, earth's surface heats up. The infrared radiation, which is shown through the red line on the right side of the Figure, emitted by the earth back in to the space thereby cooling the planet (two red arrows crossing over the atmosphere). Some of the infrared rays are trapped by the greenhouse gases in the troposphere and that is reflected back down heating the surface.[28]

The Met Office, UK also observes that in the troposphere, the rate of increase in temperature would be higher than at the earth's surface. Moreover, in the tropics, the rate of increase in temperature would be noticed mostly owing to the surface's quality of radiating the most heat.[29]

2.1.2. Climate Change: a Non-Traditional Security Threat

In views of Mely Caballero-Anthony, the non-traditional security threat is a challenge to the existence and well-beings of people, which emanates mainly out of non-traditional sources, such as climate change, environmental degradation of cross-border in nature and depletion of resources, various infectious diseases, natural disasters, severe food shortages, irregular migration, smuggling, drug trafficking, and several other forms of transnational crime.[30] These non-traditional menaces

28. "Anthropogenic Global Warming Theory", [Online: web] Accessed 24 July 2015 URL: http://www.freecriticalthinking.org/climate-change/123-anthropogenic-global-warming-theory.

29. Ibid.

30. Choudhuri, Sourabh, "Defining Non-traditional Security threats", ***Global India Foundation***, [Online: web] Accessed 12 July 2015 URL: http://www.globalindiafoundation.org/nontraditionalsecurity.html.

are much more daunting than the traditional ones. This is reflected in the deliberations in the academic circles as well as among policymakers in almost all parts of the world.

After the end of the cold war, new facets of security challenge emerged in the form of globalization, environmental degradation, and international terrorism. The nature of these newly emerged menaces and discourses on security are perpetually undergoing drastic changes that have transcended the state and military power. With the end of the cold war, a major shift in study and analysis of security and world order took place from traditional outlook to non-traditional framework.[31] With prominence the non-traditional security threats emerged mostly in developing and post-communist areas. The major factor that presumably carries the largest social, political, and economic repercussions is trade in illicit drugs.[32] However, the way climate change exerting its impact on every nook and corner of the globe is seemed to have overwhelmed all other factors contributing to the non-traditional security threat. The security obsession always exists among all countries. Connections between security intimidations and fragile political and economic performances stimulate not solely the negative development. In reality, it intimidates the very foundation of the feeble states wherein security threats flourish.[33]

Chaudhuri has postulated some attributes of the non-traditional, non-military security threat. Firstly, such issues can affect both government institutions and civilian populations. These can emerge from an assortment of non-state human and natural reasons, where the intimidation may be the outcome of certain activities done by individuals or social groups rather than the action of the states.

31. Ibid.

32. "Traditional and Non-traditional Security," ***Institute for Security & Development Policy***, [Online: web] Accessed 12 July 2015 URL: http://www.isdp.eu/issues/traditional-and-non-traditional-security.html.

33. Ibid.

Therefore, it may be assumed that the outburst of non-traditional events is more erratic. The increased mobility and pervasive individuals' activities enhance their impacts to traverse and proliferate quickly in this current world. Secondly, the effects of such issues can engender indirectly to the huge economic losses to a region or the entire world as reflected in the Financial Crisis in Asia in 1997 and the SARS (Severe Acute Respiratory Syndrome) eruption of 2002-2003.[34]

The United Nations convened Brundtland Commission, formally recognized as the *Commission on Environment and Development* (WCED) in 1983 to address the mounting concern emerged due to the burgeoning aggravation of the human environment and natural resources. This commission was also to look into the repercussion of those kinds of aggravation for economic and social development.[35] The Commission's report, *Our Common Future (*1987) discerned that problems pertaining to the environment were global in nature and extent and establishing policies for sustainable development became the common interest for all nations. The concern regarding security from climate change came out mostly from the developing world.

The international conference on climate change and security, first of its kind, took place in Toronto in 1988, was the groundbreaking event in the domain of climate change and security nexus. The several eminent scientist and policymakers attended this conference from about 50 countries. The severity of the issue related to non-traditional security was explicitly reflected in the consensus conclusion of this conference, which stated, "Humanity is conducting an unintended,

34. Choudhuri, Sourabh, "Defining Non-traditional Security threats", ***Global India Foundation***, [Online: web] Accessed 12 July 2015 URL: http://www.globalindiafoundation.org/nontraditionalsecurity.html.

35. Desai, Nitin (2010), "Climate Change: economic and historical perspectives", in The Energy and Resources Institute (eds.) ***The Environment Emergency: Exploring solutions for a sustainable future***", New Delhi: TERI Press.

uncontrolled, globally pervasive experiment whose ultimate consequences could be second only to a global nuclear war."[36]

David King in 2004 observed that people are dealing with the most severe problem of climate change today, which is more perilous even than the menaces of terrorism.[37] The United Nations Security Council (UNSC) on April 7, 2007 held their first debate on the corollary of climate change and impacts that it could have posed on peace and security of world.[38] Many member countries were however divided on the question of whether the Security Council was the right place to redress the consequences of climate change. Given the issues of climate change, many countries like China and Pakistan argued that Security Council neither had the professional competence nor is the right decision-making body.[39]It is because of the fact that climate change was primarily considered an issue of social and economic development and not a security. Nevertheless, many participants contradicted this view.[40]

Robert G. Aisi, a representative of the Papua New Guinea argued, "The impact of climate change on small islands was no less threatening than the dangerous guns and bombs posed to large nations. Pacific

---

36. ***"Our changing atmosphere: Implications for global security,"*** Secretariat of the World Meteorological Organization, conference proceedings, 27-30 June 1988. Quoted in H.L. Ferguson (2008), Twentieth Anniversary of the Toronto Conference on our changing Atmosphere: Implications for Global Security, ***Canadian Meteorological and Oceanographic Society (CMOS) Bulletin SCMO***, Vol.36, No.5, p.159; Quoted in Margaret Purdy $ Leanne Smythe (2010), From Obscurity to action: Why Canada must tackle the security dimensions of climate change, ***International Journal Spring***, p.411.

37. "Global warming 'biggest threat'," BBC News, 9 January 2004.

38. United Nations Security Council (2007), "Security Council holds first-ever debate on impact of climate change on Peace, Security, hearing over 50 speakers", [Online: web] Accessed 12 July 2015 URL: http://www.un.org/press/en/2007/sc9000.doc.htm.

39. Ibid.

40. Ibid.

island countries were likely to face massive dislocations of people, similar to population flows sparked by conflict. The impact on identity and social cohesion were likely to cause as much resentment, hatred and alienation as any refugee crisis."[41] Climate change is a problem without a passport that cannot be addressed by raising military expenditure and dispatching troops. Nor can it be controlled by sealing the borders or maintaining status quo.[42]

Climate change is not an act of terrorism; however, it will be the prime security concern of this century.[43] Mick Keelty, an Australian senior police officer, pointed out in 2007 that climate changes "have the potentials to inflict havoc, cause more deaths and pose national security issues on an unprecedented nature."[44] This statement by Keelty caught widespread public imagination. The Prime Minister of Australia, Kevin Rudd, in 2008 speech in Australian parliament, illustrated climate change as "a most fundamental national security challenge."[45] Likewise, the Center for Naval Analysis Corporation agreed to a point that climate change threats add new intimidating dimensions to the national and international security environments.[46]

41. Ibid.

42. Renner, M. (2005), "Security redefined", in L. Stark (eds.) ***State of the World 2005: redefining global security.*** Worldwatch Institute, pp. 3-19. Quoted in Maxine van Bommel (2010), Good fences don't make good neighbours: Outlining the complexities of protecting climate displaces, with special reference to India and Bangladesh", Utrecht University, p.9.

43. Walker, Jamie and Andrew Faulkner (2007), "Keelty warning on global warming," ***The Australian***, 25 September 2007, [Online: web] Accessed 12 July 2015 URL: http://www.theaustralian.com.au/archive/news/keelty-warning-on-global-warming/story-e6frg8gf-1111114495562.

44. Ibid.

45. "***The first national security statement to the Australian parliament***," address by the prime minister of Australia, December 4th 2008. Quoted in Margaret Purdy $ Leanne Smythe (2010), From Obscurity to action: Why Canada must tackle the security dimensions of climate change, ***International Journal Spring***, p.418.

46. ***"National security and the threat of climate change,"*** military advisory board, Center for Naval Analysis Corporation, 2007. Quoted in Margaret Purdy $ Leanne

Climate change issue is centre to the defense strategic maneuvers and it is being treated as the mainstream security issue by the UK government and related deployment of military forces.[47] The climate change also turned out to be a major issue in the American political discourse. President Barack Obama pointed, "The national and economic security is bound to be threatened in the long-term due to climate change. To leave the issues of climate change unchecked could turn into a violent conflict, terrible storms, shrinking coastline and irreversible catastrophe."[48]

Small Pacific islands have been susceptible to the perpetual rising trends of sea level. The intense pressure from these countries culminated into the passage of a resolution in the UN General Assembly in June 2009 that recognized unfavourable impact of climate change together with rising sea level as a "possible threat to security."[49] The Council of the European Union (2009) also raised the issue of climate change security and stated, "More vulnerable parts of human society in developing countries and emerging economies will be adversely affected, and will need our support, but developed countries will also suffer."[50]

Smythe (2010), From Obscurity to action: Why Canada must tackle the security dimensions of climate change, ***International Journal Spring***, p.416.

47. "Strategic trends programme: Future character of conflict," February 2010; and "Adaptability and partnership: Issues for the strategic defence review," green paper presented to parliament by the minister of state for defence, United Kingdom, February 2010. Quoted in Margaret Purdy $ Leanne Smythe (2010), From Obscurity to action: Why Canada must tackle the security dimensions of climate change, ***International Journal Spring***: 416-17.

48. "Obama announces plans to achieve energy independence," ***Washington Post***, January 26th 2009. [Online: web] Accessed 12 July 2015 URL:http://www.washingtonpost.com/wp-dyn/content/article/2009/01/26/AR2009012601147_2.html?sid=ST2009012601175.

49. Parsons, Claudia (2009), ***"Small islands win UN vote on climate change security," Reuters***, 3 June 2009, [Online: web] Accessed 12 July 2015 URL: http://www.reuters.com/article/2009/06/03/us-un-security-idUSTRE5525W920090603.

50. "Council conclusions on climate change and security," press release, Council of the European Union, 8 December 2009.

The impressive degree of unanimity has been seen over the implications of climate change. This could induce displacement of populations and climate migrants; slender resource and competition over water, which probably leading to conflict; fragility of state and global instability; effects on Human health, together with diffusion of diseases, and frequent onset of natural disasters. Given the wide canvas of such threats, non-traditional security deserved an independent analysis.

2.1.3. Game Theory in Realm of Climate Change Politics

Michael Finus[51] has advocated the Game theory over the issues of global warming induced climate change politics. Global emission exhibits a negative externality not only in the country of origin but also in other countries. Therefore, there is a high interdependence between countries, and strategic considerations are significant. He points out that this theory analyzes the interaction between agents. Moreover, it formulates hypotheses about their behaviour and predicts the result of the interaction. This theory also helps to explain the complications of establishing the effective and efficient cooperation. The central question that can be examined and analyzed with this theory are for instance: Under which condition will an international environmental agreement (IEA) be signed and ratified? What would be the reduction target on which signatories would agree? How many and which countries will participate in signing an agreement? Will the treaty or agreement be stable? Which measures are appropriate or may be used to give a stable shape to an IEA?[52]

Furthermore, Finus explained two frameworks of modeling international environment agreements: i) reduced stage game models

51. Finus, Michael (2002), "Game Theory and International Environemental Cooperation: Any Practical Application?" in Christoph Bohringer, Michael Finus and Carsten Vogt (eds.) ***Controlling Global Warming,*** Cheltenham, UK: Edward Elgar Publishing Limited.

52. Ibid. 2, 9.

(RSG), and ii) dynamic game models (DG model). These models are distinctively used to analyze the IEAs.

1. "RSG models consist of three stages. In the first stage, various countries decide on their membership i.e. countries decide whether and with whom they want to form a coalition. In the second stage the countries decide on the levels of emissions. A distinctive assumption, though not necessary, is that emissions are chosen cooperatively within the coalition to maximize the aggregate welfare of the coalition and towards the outsiders, coalitions behave non-cooperatively. In the final stage, coalition members decide how the aggregate welfare gain to the coalition is dispensed. The probable asymmetries, in this stage, between the coalition's members may be equalized via transfers."[53]
2. "The DG models illustrate the relations between countries as a 'true' dynamic game. Two fundamental features are cooperative in structuring these models. The first feature is whether a game is modeled as a finite or infinite game. In the case of an infinite game, there's no actual need for it to last perpetually. It is only for the fact that the end is not known with any amount of certainty. In other words, it can be said that at any given point there is a probability for the game to continue nevertheless this might be very small. The second feature is whether structural time dependency is captured which indicates that payoffs derived at some point in time bank on payoffs received and actions taken in the past."[54]

2.1.4. Non-Cooperative Theory of Emissions-Cap Determination

Shah (2004) has delineated a non-cooperative theory of emissions cap determination. He says that the contemporary international world

53. Ibid. 24.
54. Ibid.30.

is facing the problems of trans-border externalities[55] caused by the environmental pollution. The carbon externality is a global problem. Given the inability to reduce the carbon stock, Kyoto Protocol (United Nations 1997) proposes to hinder the growth of the stock of carbon by modulating fresh flow into it. However, the lack of coherence and inability of the minimal institutions to induce and monitor the compliance is conspicuously prevalent. Thus, cooperative model seems to be a failure. Hence, Shah came up with the less sanguine view of international cooperation that is non-cooperative game model of the capping stage of the protocol. This model embodies the pessimistic view that there is no mechanism for the enforcement of coalitional contracts and transfers. Consequently, an allocation of caps must be self-enforcing.[56]

This model is also different from the cooperative model in terms of nature of externality. The cooperative model shows a production externality across nations. Non-cooperative model disaggregates each nation into an emitting firm and a non-emitting consumer who are affected by the global emission externality. This model features a consumption externality. It intends to deduce the implications of an asymmetric distribution of power among the nations participating in the Protocol. Here 'Power' refers to the ability of some nations to manipulate the capping process by means of strategic choice of investment and technology. This model provides a theory of emissions cap determination in isolation from other issues.[57]

---

55. The term 'Externality' is referred to indicate the consequences of an industrial or commercial activity that is supposed to affect other people or things bereft of this being reflected in market prices. For example, pollution can be said to be a negative externality that respects no territorial boundary, and that imposes cost reduced happiness on the victims.

56. Shah, Sudhir A. (2004), "A Noncooperative Theory of Emissions –Cap Determination", in Michael A. Toman, Ujjayant Chakraborty, Shreekant Gupta (eds.) ***India and Global Climate Change: Perspective from a developing Country,*** India: Oxford University Press, pp. 259-260.

57. Ibid. 259-260.

2.1.5. Geopolitical Theory in Climate Change Politics

The term geopolitics is studied and employed in legion of diverse meanings. "It can connote a historical school of thought; a normative perspective, especially on American foreign policy; the politics of global level, which is regarded as the highest of 'high politics' that includes the geography as well. It can also be considered as a perspective that justifies the analyses of security politics in a territorial aspect, which includes the location and position of states and that accounts for the impact of geographical factors."[58] Traditionally, the theory of geopolitics has been applied as a part of realist study of international relations and politics. This theory is regarded as more policy relevant than the realist approach. The term 'Geopolitics' was coined by Swedish political scientist, Rudolf Members who explained geopolitics as a concept that elucidates the policy of a state expressing it through a natural geographical factors, geographical location and identification of geographic entities.[59]Keller defined geopolitics as the theory of the state, which is a geographic-spatial phenomenon. To him, the notion of state presumes somewhat territorially and geographically substantive existing entity.[60]

Spasov has pointed out how the negative impact of climate change has drawn global geopolitical implications. He defined geopolitics as a "social science discipline concerned with studying the mutual relationship between the ethnic, demographic and economic aspects of the impact of political relations in a country."[61] Climate change is a global phenomenon affecting almost all fundamental areas of the

58. Halden, Peter (2007), "***The Geopolitics of Climate change: Challenges to the international System***",stockholm: Swedish Defence Research Agency. P. 43-44.

59. Spasov, MA Nikolco."Global Geopolitical Implications for the World As A Result of the Negative Impacts of Climate Change", ***Scientific Article***, 551.583 (100), p.3.

60. Halden, Peter (2007), "***The Geopolitics of Climate change: Challenges to the international System***",stockholm: Swedish Defence Research Agency, p. 44.

61. Spasov, MA Nikolco."Global Geopolitical Implications for the World As A Result of the Negative Impacts of Climate Change", ***Scientific Article***, 551.583 (100), pp.1-10.

planet and humanity. The significance of embedding climate change in the realm of geopolitical analysis comes to the limelight when one ponders over the future cost of climate change on particular regions and strategic directions that would alter the power of geopolitics in the world. These considerations rely on geographical power, which is derived from global changes that changes the environment today.[62]

Murthy and Hommel[63] observed that Mackinder's 1904 address on "The Geographical Pivot of History" to the Royal Geographical society, opened up a new way of thinking about the complex interactions among geography, politics, and power. Mackinder argued that geographical and environmental factors such as distance, climate and topography would affect the future balance of power. For Mackinder, the geographical positions and abundance of natural resources are the prime factors in determining the power and foreign policy of a country. Stressing so much on the Eurasian pivot area that later came to be known as the Heartland, he considered this region as the "natural seat of power."[64] To him, the natural seat of power like region might allow an imperial power like Britain to become "the empire of the world."[65] The idea of the Mackinder was to encourage speculation about the relevance of geography and environment in geopolitics at a time when environmental change has taken the centre stage among the issues of global concern.[66]

62. Ibid. 1-10.

63. Murthy, Alexander B. and Demian Hommel, "The Geopolitical Implications of Environmental Change", University of Oregon, Eugene, Oregon: USA. pp. 2-3.

64. Mackinder, H. J. (1904), "The Geographical Pivot of History." ***The Geographical Journal***, 23 (4): 421-442. Quoted in Murthy, Alexander B. and Demian Hommel, "The Geopolitical Implications of Environmental Change", University of Oregon, Eugene, Oregon: USA, p.2.

65. Ibid.2.

66. Spasov, MA Nikolco:"Global Geopolitical Implications for the world as a result of the Negative Impacts of Climate Change", ***Scientific Article***, 551.583 (100), p.3; Murthy, Alexander B. and Demian Hommel, "The Geopolitical Implications of Environmental Change", University of Oregon, Eugene, Oregon: USA. pp. 3-4.

Mackinder observed that the all-great wars of history have the outcome, directly or indirectly, of the uneven growth of nations, because of the asymmetric allocation of fertility and strategical chances in the wake of the global climate change. The very term 'fertility' implies the 'agriculture,' which, to the large extent, is a climate dependent matter.[67]

Nicholas Spykman extended the approach of geopolitical to world affairs during the early 1940s. He argued that international society is "a society without a central authority to preserve law and order and without an official agency to protect its members."[68] Furthermore, he stated that geopolitics is an analysis of the interconnectedness between realist theory and geographical factors, and he regarded geography as the most vital component that forms the foreign policy in a world of anarchy, in view of its permanency.[69] Taking different position than several other scholars, Spykman said that no geopolitical regions in the world are determined alone by the geography; but also by the changing dynamics of the balance of power. Hence, his geopolitical analysis deals with the dynamic situation rather than a static.[70]

According to Spykman, as analysed by Halden, topography, in the first place, plays the vital role to fix the ease or difficulty with which

---

67. Mackinder, H.J. (1919/1996), "Democratic Ideals and Reality: A Study in the Politics of Reconstruction", Washington, DC: National Defense University Press, pp.1-3; Halden, Peter (2007), "The Geopolitics of Climate change: Challenges to the International System", FOI, Swedish Defence Research Agency, Stockholm,Sweden, p.46.

68. Spykman, N.J. (1942), ***"America's Strategy in World Politics: The United States and the balance of Power",*** New York: Harcourt, Brace, p.7; Halden, Peter (2007), "The Geopolitics of Climate change: Challenges to the International System", ***FOI, Swedish Defence Research Agency***, Stockholm, Sweden, p.45.

69. Halden, Peter (2007), "The Geopolitics of Climate change: Challenges to the International System", ***FOI, Swedish Defence Research Agency***, Stockholm, Sweden, p.45; Spykman, N.J. (1942), ***"America's Strategy in World Politics: The United States and the balance of Power",*** New York: Harcourt, Brace, p.41.

70. Spykman, N.J. (1944), "***The Geography of the Peace***", New York: Harcourt, Brace and Campany, p.6.

one can trade or defend one's border. In the second place, the economic structure of a state is conditioned by the climate of that country and that climate, which is indirectly in a way, determines the state's foreign policy. It is just like the climate factors affecting transportation and limits agricultural productivity.[71] Moreover, Halden in his report on the *'geopolitics of climate change'* has applied the concept of 'pivotal states' to denote a state whose regional significance is so paramount that changes in it will have reverberations throughout the region. Danial Esty has attached the issues of environmental degradation to concept of pivotal states.[72] In the analysis of Esty, the older notion of 'pivotal states' meant, a state having position to maintain the regional or even global balance of power. The effects of environmental degradation can have on the stability of some states known to be 'pivot.'[73] In other words, it means that environmental degradation can affect the stability of a state.

This study focuses on the impact of climate change on Sundarbans and its implications for India -Bangladesh relations that constitute the vital aspects of geopolitics between both the nations. Given the fact that Sundarbans shares its geographical boundary with both countries, India and Bangladesh, the geo-politics of environmental management in the context of climate change is emerging to be rather critical. The abundance of natural resource is on the brink of depletion due to the man-made anthropogenic activities and natural climate change

71. Halden, Peter (2007), "The Geopolitics of Climate change: Challenges to the International System", ***FOI, Swedish Defence Research Agency***, Stockholm, Sweden, p.47.

72. Esty, Daniel C (1999), "Pivotal States and the Environment" in Robert Chase, Emily Hill and Paul Kennedy (eds.) ***The Pivotal States: A New Framework for US Policy in the Developing World***, New York: W.W.Nortan and Company pp.298-299. Quoted in Halden, Peter (2007), "The Geopolitics of Climate change: Challenges to the International System", ***FOI, Swedish Defence Research Agency***, Stockholm, Sweden, p.48.

73. Ibid.48.

impacts. Any damage in one part can affect the other. This can even induce destabilization and trigger security threats.

The next section deals with the nature, contents, dimensions and implications of climate change in general. The observed impacts of changing nature of climate and projected impacts in future have been given attention. In this section, the focus has also been shifted on whether the phenomenon of climate change is global and real in terms of its reach and impact. This section is largely contingent on the material and facts extracted from Fifth Assessment Report of Intergovernmental Panel on Climate Change (IPCC) 2014, Asian Development Bank (2014),Greenhouse Effect and its Impact on the Region (1992) prepared by SAARC Secretariat.

2.2. Nature, Contents, Dimensions and Implications of Climate Change: global to regional

The phenomenon of climate change is global and real in nature, and has already begun to have serious impacts on all aspects of socio-ecological systems around the world. In the recent years, there has been a lot of discussion on the issues of nature and implications of climate change around the world. The changing nature and impacts of climate change can be studied in terms of observed and projected changes in temperature, hydrological cycle, extreme weather events, and changes in sea level rise.

2.2.1. Changes in Temperature

The increased concentration of the greenhouse gas[74] (GHG) in the

74. According to the Oxford dictionary, the term 'greenhouse gas' denotes any of the gases that are supposed to cause the greenhouse effect, especially carbon dioxide. It is believed that "large scale of anthropogenic activities, involving those of combustion of fossil fuels lead to increases in the GHS" (Chinnamai et al. 2011: 11). In other words, "Greenhouse gases are that kind of gas that absorbs and emits (reflects back) infrared radition in the wavelength range emitted by earth" (Accessed 17 July 2015 URL: https://en.wikipedia.org/wiki/Greenhouse_gas). The major GHSs that contribute to the climate change are carbon dioxide(CO_2), methane(CH4), nitrous oxide(N2O), hydrofluorocarbons (HFCs), per fluorocarbon (PFCs), and sulfur hexafluoride (SF6),

atmosphere has resulted in enhanced greenhouse effect[75] leading to climate change.[76] IPCC *Fourth Assessment Report* states that the emission of heat trapping gas from human activities have resulted in most of the observed increase in average temperature globally.[77] IPCC assessed that since the 19th century Global Mean Surface Temperature (GMST) has increased. The first decade of the twenty first century has been the warmest.[78]

On a global average, temperatures have increased from 0.3°C to 0.6°C between the late nineteenth century and 1994 and the full range of projected temperature rise is 1.1°C to 6.4°C by the end of

---

water vapor(H2O) and Ozone(O3) (Chinnamai et al. 2011: 11; and URL: https://en.wikipedia.org/wiki/Greenhouse_gas). Moreover, It is observed that 95% of the greenhouse gas is water vapour, whereas the extent of carbon dioxide is relatively as minor constituent that makes a marginal contribution to the greenhouse system ("Are rising man-made CO2 emissions causing global warming", online: web, Accessed 24 July 2015 URL: http://www.freecriticalthinking.org/climate-change/124-are-rising-man-made-co2-emissions-are-causing-global-warming).

75. The Oxford dictionary defines Greenhouse effect as a problem related to the gradual increase in temperature of the earth's atmosphere, which is caused by an increase of gases such as carbon dioxide in the air surrounding the earth that traps the heat of the Sun. In other words, "the greenhouse effect is a process through which a planetary surface gets warmed by radiation from its atmosphere to a temperature above what it would be in absence of its atmosphere. If a planets's atmosphere retains radiatively active gases that is greenhouse gases, the atmosphere radiates energy in all directions and the part of this radiation is directed towards the surface making it warm. Increasing human activities strengthen the greenhouse effect, which is commonly known as the enhanced (or anthropogenic) greenhouse effect" (Accessed 17 July 2015 URL: https://en.wikipedia.org/wiki/Greenhouse_effect).

76. Chinnamai, A. Mariyappan, and M. Selvaraj (2011), "Mitigating Climate change: the Indian Perspective", ***The Research Journal of Sherubtse College***, p.11.

77. Ibid.11.

78. Hartmann, D.L. et al (2013), "Observations: Atmosphere and Surface", in Stocker, T.F., D. Qin, G.-K. Plattner, M. Tignor, S.K. Allen, J. Boschung, A. Nauels, Y. Xia, V. Bex and P.M. Midgley (eds.) ***Climate Change 2013: The Physical Science Basis. Contribution of Working Group I to the Fifth Assessment Report of the Intergovernmental Panel on Climate,*** Cambridge: Cambridge University Press, p.161.

this century.[79] The natural range that existed over 650,000 years is exceeded by the concentration of carbon dioxide in 2005.[80] Evidence from observations of the climate system showed an increase of 0.095 ± 0.020°C per decade in global average Land-surface Air Temperature (LSAT) during the 111 year period from 1901 to 2012.[81] The warming trend over the 61 years period from 1951 to 2012 has been 0.175 ± 0.037°C per decade; and 0.254 ± 0.050°C per decade between years 1979 and 2012.[82] The globally averaged maximum and minimum temperature over land have both accelerated by in excess of 0.1°C per decade since 1950.[83]

The global average sea surface temperatures (SST) have increased since the beginning of the twentieth century. It has been 0.052 ± 0.007°C per decade from period 1901 to 2012. Warming trends of global sea surface temperature in comparison to the entire 111-year periods has increased to 0.072°C ± 0.024°C per decade during the period of 1979-

---

79. Chinnamai, A. Mariyappan, and M. Selvaraj (2011), "Mitigating Climate change: the Indian Perspective", ***The Research Journal of Sherubtse College***, p.11

80. Sivakumar, Mannava V.K. and Robert Stefanski, "Climate change in South Asia" Chapter 2, p.16, [Online: web] Accessed 17 July 2015 URL: file:///C:/Users/Prashant%20Kr.%20Sharma/Downloads/9789048195152-c2.pdf.

81. Jones, P. D. et al. (2012), "Hemispheric and large-scale land-surface air temperature variations: An extensive revision and an update to 2010", ***J. Geophys. Res. Atmos.***, 117,D05127. Quoted in Hartmann, D.L. et al (2013), "Observations: Atmosphere and Surface", in Stocker, T.F., D. Qin, G.-K. Plattner, M. Tignor, S.K. Allen, J. Boschung, A. Nauels, Y. Xia, V. Bex and P.M. Midgley (eds.) ***Climate Change 2013: The Physical Science Basis. Contribution of Working Group I to the Fifth Assessment Report of the Intergovernmental Panel on Climate,*** Cambridge: Cambridge University Press, p.187.

82. Ibid.187

83. Hartmann, D.L. et al (2013), "Observations: Atmosphere and Surface", in Stocker, T.F., D. Qin, G.-K. Plattner, M. Tignor, S.K. Allen, J. Boschung, A. Nauels, Y. Xia, V. Bex and P.M. Midgley (eds.) ***Climate Change 2013: The Physical Science Basis. Contribution of Working Group I to the Fifth Assessment Report of the Intergovernmental Panel on Climate,*** Cambridge: Cambridge University Press, p.188.

2012.[84] Another observation shows increasing trends of 0.124 $\pm$ 0.030°C per decade from 1979 to 2012.[85] Land surface regions have become warm at a faster rate than the ocean. Warming has been found in both land and ocean domains and both in sea surface temperature (SST) and nighttime marine air temperature over the oceans. Surface air temperatures have risen globally over the land at about double the ocean rate after 1979 (more than 0.27° C per decade vs. 0.13°C per decade).[86]

According to the IPCC Fifth Assessment Report, "it is very likely that mean annual temperature has increased over the past century over most of the region of Asia. It is very likely too that the numbers of warm days and nights have increased across most of Asia since about 1950. The frequency of heat wave has increased since the middle of the twentieth century in large parts of Asia."[87]Moreover, "With an increase of 2.4°C in the mid latitude

84. Rayner, N. A., et al. (2003) Global analyses of sea surface temperature, sea ice, and night marine air temperature since the late nineteenth century. ***J. Geophys. Res. Atmos.***, 108, 37. Quoted in Hartmann, D.L. et al (2013), "Observations: Atmosphere and Surface", in Stocker, T.F., D. Qin, G.-K. Plattner, M. Tignor, S.K. Allen, J. Boschung, A. Nauels, Y. Xia, V. Bex and P.M. Midgley (eds.) ***Climate Change 2013: The Physical Science Basis. Contribution of Working Group I to the Fifth Assessment Report of the Intergovernmental Panel on Climate,*** Cambridge: Cambridge University Press, p.192.

85. Kennedy, J. J. et al.(2011) Reassessing biases and other uncertainties in sea surface temperature observations measured in situ since 1850: 2. Biases and homogenization. ***J. Geophys. Res. Atmos.,*** 116, D14104. Quoted in Hartmann, D.L. et al (2013), "Observations: Atmosphere and Surface", in Stocker, T.F., D. Qin, G.-K. Plattner, M. Tignor, S.K. Allen, J. Boschung, A. Nauels, Y. Xia, V. Bex and P.M. Midgley (eds.) ***Climate Change 2013: The Physical Science Basis. Contribution of Working Group I to the Fifth Assessment Report of the Intergovernmental Panel on Climate,*** Cambridge: Cambridge University Press, p.190.

86. Sivakumar, Mannava V.K. and Robert Stefanski, "Climate change in South Asia" Chapter 2, p.17, [Online: web] Accessed 17 July 2015 URL: file:///C:/Users/Prashant%20Kr.%20Sharma/Downloads/9789048195152-c2.pdf.

87. IPCC (2014) ***Climate Change 2014: Impacts, Adaptation, and Vulnerability. Part B: Regional Aspects. Contribution of Working Group II to the Fifth Assessment***

semi-arid area of Asia, the warming trend was observed particularly strong in the season of cold between November and March over the period of 1909 to 2009. The increasing annual mean temperature trends at the country scale in South Asia have been observed during the twentieth century."[88] A report published by Asian Development Bank also expresses its concern over the changing phenomena of climate that it may pose to the South Asian countries.[89]

"Climate change will affect South Asia more than most other regions. Weather of South Asia is likely to become hotter than the global average, while monsoonal rains and heavy storms will increase in most parts of this region. As well, the mountainous countries face increased flooding and landslides, while the coastal countries of this region are likely to be partly inundated by sea-level rise."[90]

Report of the Intergovernmental Panel on Climate Change [Barros, V.R.,C.B. Field, D.J. Dokken, M.D. Mastrandrea, K.J. Mach, T.E. Bilir, M. Chatterjee,K.L. Ebi, Y.O. Estrada, R.C. Genova, B. Girma, E.S. Kissel, A.N. Levy, S. MacCracken,P.R. Mastrandrea, and L.L. White (eds.)]. Cambridge University Press, Cambridge, United Kingdom and New York, NY, USA, pp. 1333.

88. Ibid. 1333

89. Asian Development Bank (2014), ***"Climate Action South Asia: Steering Economics Towards low Carbon and Climate resilient development"*** CASA Information Update, No.5.

90. Ibid.

Table: 2.1. Summary of major observed past and present climate trends and variability in some South Asian countries[91]

Country	Changes in Temperature	Changes in precipitation
Bangla-desh	Increasing trend of temperature of about 1°C in May and 0.5°C in November from 1985 to 1998	Decadal rain anomalies above long term averages since 1960s
India	0.68°C increase per century with increasing pattern in annual mean temperature and warming getting more pronounced during post monsoon and winter	Increase in extreme level rains in northwest during summer monsoon in recent decades and lower number of rainy days along east coast
Nepal	0.09°C increase per year in Himalayas and 0.04°C in Terai region with more in winter	No distinct long-term patterns in precipitation records for 1948–1994
Pakistan	Since early 1990s in coastal areas 0.6–1.0°C increase in mean temperature	10–15% decrease in precipitation in coastal belt and hyper arid plains and increase in summer and winter precipitation over the last 40 years in northern Pakistan
Sri Lanka	0.016°C increase per year between 1961 to 90 over entire country and 2°C increase per year in central highlands	An increasing pattern in February and decreasing pattern in June

91. Cruz RV et al. (2007) Asia, Climate change, 2007, impacts, adaptation and vulnerability. In: Parry ML,

Canziani OF, Palutikof JP et al (eds) Contribution of Working Group II to the Fourth Assessment Report of the Intergovernmental Panel on Climate Change. Cambridge UniversityPress, Cambridge, pp 469–506. Quoted in Sivakumar, Mannava V.K. and Robert Stefanski, "Climate change in South Asia" Chapter 2, p.17, [Online: web] Accessed 17 July 2015 URL: file:///C:/Users/Prashant%20Kr.%20Sharma/Downloads/9789048195152-c2.pdf.

The statement enumerated above shows the vulnerability of countries due to the climate change. South Asia is known to be the most disaster prone region in the world, which is home to over one fifth of the world's population.[92] The six developing member countries (DMCs) of South Asia –Bangladesh, Bhutan, India, Maldives, Nepal, and Sri Lanka – of the Asian Development Bank (ADB) are "home to about 1.5 billion people nearly a third of whom are still living in poverty." The severe impact of climate change will make the life of these people even trickier to come out of the poverty.[93]

The above given Table 2.1 depicts that past and present climate patterns and variability in South Asia in general can be portrayed by the increasing air temperature. For South Asia, temperature projections for the 21st century indicate a major rise in warming over that observed in the 20th century.[94] The observed increases in temperature during these recent decades in some parts of Asia have varied between less than 1-3°C per century.[95] In Bangladesh, increasing trend of temperature has been observed of about 1°C during the month of May and 0.5°C in the month of November. As far as India is concerned, an increasing trend in annual mean temperature with 0.68°C per century has been observed as it is clearly pointed out in the Table 2.1.

In terms of agriculture, some regions of South Asia may benefit from the future warmer temperature. However, the overall impact of climate change on agriculture is anticipated to be negative, which is posing a serious threat to the food security in this region. For instance, in Bhutan and India early gains are predicted in rice that may decline

92. Sivakumar, Mannava V.K. and Robert Stefanski, "Climate change in South Asia" Chapter 2, p.13, [Online: web] Accessed 17 July 2015 URL: file:///C:/Users/Prashant%20Kr.%20Sharma/Downloads/9789048195152-c2.pdf.

93. Ibid.

94. Sivakumar, Mannava V.K. and Robert Stefanski, "Climate change in South Asia" Chapter 2, p.13, [Online: web] Accessed 17 July 2015 URL: file:///C:/Users/Prashant%20Kr.%20Sharma/Downloads/9789048195152-c2.pdf.

95. Ibid.17

again by the 2050s. In Nepal's hill and mountains, the production of rice is expected to increase by 2080s by as much as 16%. On the other hand, in the extensive tropical and sub-tropical regions of Bangladesh, Bhutan, India, and Sri Lanka, there is possibility of decline in agriculture as much as 23%.[96]

2.2.2. Changes in Hydrological Cycle

With the projection of increase in global temperature, it is commonly agreed that the global hydrological cycle will become intense leading to extreme droughts and floods becoming more frequent, and this is highlighted by the IPCC in its assessments of the susceptibility of regional impacts of the climate change.[97] Changing hydrological cycle will have its impacts on the quantity, quality, timing, and distribution of rain, evaporation, and the runoff.

2.2.2.1. Changing patterns of precipitation

"The changing rainfall pattern will largely affect the distribution of world agriculture. Most of the countries that have endured the brunt of increase or decrease in monthly or seasonal precipitation have also sustained a disproportionate change in the amount of precipitation falling during the heavy and extreme events. In Japan, for instance, there was no increase in the seasonal precipitation, however frequency of one-day heavy precipitation events was still found to be increasing."[98]

In the South Asian region, the frequency of heavy precipitation events is observed to be increasing, while light rain events are

96. Asian Development Bank (2014), ***"Climate Action South Asia: Steering Economics Towards low Carbon and Climate resilient development"*** CASA Information Update, No.5.

97. Watson R.T. et al. (eds.) (1998), ***The regional impacts of climate change: An assessment of vulnerability,*** Cambridge: Cambridge University Press.

98. Mishra, A.K. et al. (2010), "Impact of global warming and climate change on social development", ***Journal of Comparative social welfare***, 26:2-3, 239-260.

decreasing.[99] In India, an extreme level rains is observed to be increasing in northwest during summer monsoon in recent decades. The above given Table 2.1 provides a detailed list on observed trends of rainfall for some of the South Asian countries.

2.2.2.2. Impacts on water resources

Water resources are closely linked with climate. The possibility of global climate change will impinge upon the water resources and regional development.[100]Climate change led changing precipitation would also have its effects on the quality and quantity of fresh water concerning the drinking water, sanitation, agriculture, and industrial requirements. The intensive irrigation will be needed in certain areas because of the steep evaporation caused by higher global average temperature.[101]

The World Meteorological Organization (1997) gauged that approximately one-third population of the world residing in those countries was deemed to be the victims of water stress. Furthermore, the assessment estimated that by 2025 more than two third population of the world would be residing in water stressed countries. Climate change will exacerbate the water stress, inducing further stresses on supplies of water.[102]

---

99. IPCC (2014) ***Climate Change 2014: Impacts, Adaptation, and Vulnerability. Part B: Regional Aspects. Contribution of Working Group II to the Fifth Assessment Report of the Intergovernmental Panel on Climate Change*** [Barros, V.R.,C.B. Field, D.J. Dokken, M.D. Mastrandrea, K.J. Mach, T.E. Bilir, M. Chatterjee,K.L. Ebi, Y.O. Estrada, R.C. Genova, B. Girma, E.S. Kissel, A.N. Levy, S. MacCracken,P.R. Mastrandrea, and L.L. White (eds.)]. Cambridge University Press, Cambridge, United Kingdom and New York, NY, USA, p. 1333.

100. Riebsame WE, et al. (1995) Complex river basins. In: Strzepek KM, Smith JB (eds) As climate changes, international impacts and implications. Cambridge University Press, Cambridge, pp 57–91. Quoted in Sivakumar, Mannava V.K. and Robert Stefanski, "Climate change in South Asia" Chapter 2, p.23, [Online: web] Accessed 17 July 2015 URL: file:///C:/Users/Prashant%20Kr.%20Sharma/Downloads/9789048195152-c2.pdf.

101. Mishra, A.K. et al. (2010), "Impact of global warming and climate change on social development", ***Journal of Comparative social welfare***, 26:2-3, 239-260

102. Ibid.

The region of South Asia is endowed with great rivers that are the major source of the regional economy. The mountain range of the Himalayan-Hindu Kush covered with the ice mass is the source of the nine largest rivers of Asia, encompassing the Ganges, Brahmaputra, and Indus. More than half of the world's population is provided water by these rivers. In Asia, most people are reliant on the glacial melt water throughout dry season. The rapid trend of glacial melt due to the climate change impact thwarts the very continuing nature of several Himalayan originated rivers. This is likely to impinge upon those people who rely on the resource affecting availability of water for agricultural purposes.[103] In Nepal and Bhutan, melting trends of glaciers are observed to be filling glacial lakes exceeding their capacities culminating into Glacial Lake Outburst Floods (GLOFs).[104] Concerning the GLOFs in Nepal, 20 out of 2,323 glacial lakes have been reported to be possibly perilous.[105]

In the South Asian region, especially in Bangladesh, Bhutan, Nepal, and Sri Lanka, the supply of water is estimated to remain higher owing partly to the positive effects of increasing rainfall. On the other hand, due to the variations in the degree of intensity and rainfall distribution, South Asia as a whole will sustain water deficit. Water deficit is expected to be observed mostly in India. Water deficit in India

---

103. Kelkar U and Bhadwal S (2007) ***South Asian regional study on climate change impacts and adaptation: implications for human development.*** Human Development Report Office, Occasional Paper. United Nations Development Programme. Quoted in Sivakumar, Mannava V.K. and Robert Stefanski, "Climate change in South Asia" Chapter 2, p.23, [Online: web] Accessed 17 July 2015 URL: file:///C:/Users/Prashant%20Kr.%20Sharma/Downloads/9789048195152-c2.pdf.

104. UNEP (2007) ***GEO yearbook 2007: an overview of our changing environment,.*** UNEP, Nairobi, p 86. Quoted in Sivakumar, Mannava V.K. and Robert Stefanski, "Climate change in South Asia" Chapter 2, p.23, [Online: web] Accessed 17 July 2015 URL: file:///C:/Users/Prashant%20Kr.%20Sharma/Downloads/9789048195152-c2.pdf.

105. Ibid.23

will be roughly 300 billion cubic meters (m3) and 400 billion m3 by 2030 and 2050s respectively.[106]

2.2.2.3. Extreme weather events

IPCC *Fifth Assessment Report* estimated, "it is very likely that the numbers of cold days and nights have decreased and the numbers of warm days and nights have increased globally since about 1950." Due to the lack of sufficient data or of studies on extreme weather events in Africa and South America, there is only medium confidence that the length and frequency of warm spells, together with the heat waves, has increased since middle of the twentieth century.[107]

Furthermore, this report depicts the likelihood that "since about 1950 the number of heavy precipitation events over land has increased in more regions than it has decreased. For North America and Europe, confidence is highest where there have been likely increases in either the frequency or intensity of heavy precipitation with some seasonal and /or regional variation. Moreover, it is very likely that there have been trends towards heavier precipitation events in Central America."[108]

Extreme events engender the frequent occurrence of floods that results in the massive devastation ofhumankind. An increase in amount, intensity, and extension of precipitation with increase in temperature leads to the occurrence of frequent floods. Douben delineated that about 65% of the floods are triggered by heavy and/or long lasting rainfall, 15% by short torrential rainfall, 10% by tropical cyclones, and

---

106. Asian Development Bank (2014), ***"Climate Action South Asia: Steering Economics Towards low Carbon and Climate resilient development"*** CASA Information Update, No.5.

107. Hartmann, D.L. et al (2013), "Observations: Atmosphere and Surface", in Stocker, T.F., D. Qin, G.-K. Plattner, M. Tignor, S.K. Allen, J. Boschung, A. Nauels, Y. Xia, V. Bex and P.M. Midgley (eds.) ***Climate Change 2013: The Physical Science Basis. Contribution of Working Group I to the Fifth Assessment Report of the Intergovernmental Panel on Climate,*** Cambridge: Cambridge University Press, p.162.

108. Ibid. 162

5% by monsoonal rains.[109] South Asia is a region that experiences an exceptionally greater number of natural disasters. It is observed that "between 1990 and 2008, more than 750 million people (50% of this region's population) were affected by a natural disaster that left almost 60,000 dead and resulting in about $45 billion in damages."[110] For instance, cyclone Sidr in 2007, Nargis in 2008, Aila in 2009 and Laila in 2010 were the annual extreme weather events among a number of other disasters.[111] Cyclone Aila of 2009 was one of the most dramatic of the climatic disasters to have lately hit the Sundarbans,[112] and that left over 2.3 million people displaced and nearly 8,000 missing between India and Bangladesh.[113]

Climate Change impact added with the anthropogenic impact will also have a huge effect upon the forest resources in tropical zones. The anthropogenic factors will include changes in land use patterns and deforestation. The impact of climate change is likely to be extremely important in tropical region. The mangrove forests do not remain an exception to these changes anymore. Along the Indus delta, the mangrove forests in Pakistan, particularly a diverse ecosystem, will experience the brunt of climate change.[114]

---

109. Douben, K.J. (2006), "Characteristic of river floods and flooding: A global overview, 1985-2003", ***Irrigation and Drainage***, 55 (S1), S9-S21.

110. Sivakumar, Mannava V.K. and Robert Stefanski, "Climate change in South Asia" Chapter 2, p.24, [Online: web] Accessed 17 July 2015 URL: file:///C:/Users/Prashant%20Kr.%20Sharma/Downloads/9789048195152-c2.pdf.

111. Musa, A.R.M.A. (2010), "Latest news on climate displacement in Bangladesh: Displacement Solutions", [Online: web] Accessed 7 March 2015, URL: http://displacementsolutions.org/latest-news-on-climate-displacement-in-bangladesh/.

112. Danda et al. (2010), "Sundarbans: Future Imperfect- Climate Adaptation Report", ***WWF Report India***, p.11.

113. Dhar, Sujoy (2009***), "Hungry Tides in India's Sunderbans" Aljazeera,*** 14th December. Quoted in Shloka Nath (2011***), "Environmental Diplamacy: Saving the Sunderbans and Restoring Indo-Bangladesh Friendship"***, Mumbai: Gateway House: Indian Council on Global Relations, p.42.

114. Zhao Y, Wang C, Wang S, Tibig L (2005) Impacts of present and future climate variability on agriculture and forestry in the humid and sub-humid

Extreme weather events also lead a number of incidences of draughts that can have significant social, economic, and ecological impacts. It is a wide spread phenomenon. Almost one-half of the Earth's terrestrial surfaces are vulnerable to draughts.[115] Warming of temperature could induce draughts that could result in the "loss of 40% of the Amazon, turning it into a carbon producer, through decay of dead vegetation, from its current role as a carbon sink or absorber."[116] On the problem of draughts, the IPCC has expressed a low confidence "for a global-scale observed trend in drought or dryness (lack of rainfall) since the middle of the twentieth century, due to the dearth of direct observations, methodological uncertainties and geographical inconsistencies in the trends."[117] Due to the increased number and severity of draughts, the losses throughout the world have also increased significantly.[118] At the regional level, the frequency and intensity of draught have been observed to be soaring in the Mediterranean and West Africa, nevertheless, decreasing trends observed since 1950 in central North America and north-west Australia.[119]

---

tropics. Climatic Change 70:73–116. Quoted in Sivakumar, Mannava V.K. and Robert Stefanski, "Climate change in South Asia" Chapter 2, p.26, [Online: web] Accessed 17 July 2015 URL: file:///C:/Users/Prashant%20Kr.%20Sharma/Downloads/9789048195152-c2.pdf.

115. Korgan, F.N. (1997), "Global draught watch from space", ***Bulletin of the American Meteorological society***, 78: 621-636.

116. Kintisch, E. (2009), "Projections of climate change go from bad to worse, Scientist report", ***Science***, No.323: 1546-1547.

117. Hartmann, D.L. et al (2013), "Observations: Atmosphere and Surface", in Stocker, T.F., D. Qin, G.-K. Plattner, M. Tignor, S.K. Allen, J. Boschung, A. Nauels, Y. Xia, V. Bex and P.M. Midgley (eds.) ***Climate Change 2013: The Physical Science Basis. Contribution of Working Group I to the Fifth Assessment Report of the Intergovernmental Panel on Climate,*** Cambridge: Cambridge University Press, p.162.

118. Wilhite, D.A. (2000), "Draught as a natural hazard: Concepts and definitions", in D.A. Wilhite (eds) ***Draught: A global assessment***, pp.3-18, Natural Hazards and Disasters series, London: Routledge Publishers.

119. Hartmann, D.L. et al (2013), "Observations: Atmosphere and Surface", in Stocker, T.F., D. Qin, G.-K. Plattner, M. Tignor, S.K. Allen, J. Boschung, A. Nauels,

2.2.3. Changes in Sea Level Rise and its Impact

The phenomenon of sea level change is one of the major attributes of the observed climate change impact that could pose an existential threat to the countries adjacent to the sea. "Climate change is taking place and will cause sea level to rise for centuries even if greenhouse gas emissions are stabilized."[120] Ocean thermal expansions are largely responsible for the sea level rise that expands existing water, and melting of glacier mostly from the Greenland and Antarctica adding water to the oceans.[121] IPCC *Fifth Assessment Report* also observed that ocean thermal expansion and glacier melt have been the leading contributors to the twentieth century global rise in mean sea level.[122]

IPCC stated that observations since 1971 point out that thermal expansions and glaciers (excluding Antarctica glaciers peripheral to the ice sheet) present 75% of the observed rise. Since the early 1990s, the contribution of the Greenland and Antarctica ice sheets has increased, partly from increased outflow induced by warming of the immediately adjacent ocean.[123] IPCC in its "Third Assessment Report (2001)

Y. Xia, V. Bex and P.M. Midgley (eds.) ***Climate Change 2013: The Physical Science Basis. Contribution of Working Group I to the Fifth Assessment Report of the Intergovernmental Panel on Climate,*** Cambridge: Cambridge University Press, p.162.

120. Smith, Anthony Oliver (2009), "Sea Level Rise and the Vulnerability of Coastal Peoples: Responding to the Local Challenges of Global Climate Change in the 21st Century", ***United Nations University-UNU-EHS-Institute for Environment and Human Security***, No.7/2009:17.

121. Hemming, D. et al. (2007), ***"Impacts of Mean Sea Level Rise Based on current state of the Art Modelling"***, Hadley Centre for Climate Prediction and Research, Exeter, UK. Quoted in Smith, Anthony Oliver (2009), "Sea Level Rise and the Vulnerability of Coastal Peoples: Responding to the Local Challenges of Global Climate Change in the 21st Century", ***United Nations University-UNU-EHS-Institute for Environment and Human Security***, No.7/2009:18.

122. Church, J.A. et al. (2013), "Sea Level Change", in Stocker,T.F. et al. (eds.) ***Climate Change 2013: The Physical Science Basis.*** Contribution of Working Group I to the Fifth Assessment Report of the Intergovernmental Panel on Climate Change, Cambridge: Cambridge University Press, p.1139.

123. Ibid.1139.

predicted that sea level will rise approximately one meter in the twenty first century."[124] The IPCC *Fourth Assessment Report* (2007) estimated rises in sea level up to 0.6 meters or more by 2100.[125]

IPCC's *Special Report on Emissions Scenarios* pointed out that global mean sea level rise ranges from 22 cm to 34 cm, between 1990 and 2080s.[126] IPCC in its *Fifth Assessment Report* stated that global rise in mean sea level will persist beyond 2100, along with the rise in sea level that is supposed to keep on for many centuries owing to the thermal expansion, and the longer-term degree of increases in the level of sea will rest on the level of future emissions.[127]

The physical exposure to sea level rise seems to perpetually becoming the matter of concern for those countries adjoining to the sea. The possibility of great devastation emanates from the fact that historically, human settlements have always been located within 100 miles of coastal or areas of riverine with the purpose of production and exchange.[128] At present, 10% of the global population that is 600

124. IPCC (2001), "Climate Change 2001:Impacts, Adaptation and Vulnerability", J. J. McCarthy, O. F. Canziani, N. A. Leary, D. J. Dokken and K. S. White (eds.), Cambridge: Cambridge University Press. Quoted in Smith, Anthony Oliver (2009), "Sea Level Rise and the Vulnerability of Coastal Peoples: Responding to the Local Challenges of Global Climate Change in the 21st Century", ***United Nations University-UNU-EHS-Institute for Environment and Human Security***, No.7/2009:18.

125. Smith, Anthony Oliver (2009), "Sea Level Rise and the Vulnerability of Coastal Peoples: Responding to the Local Challenges of Global Climate Change in the 21st Century", ***United Nations University-UNU-EHS-Institute for Environment and Human Security***, No.7/2009:18.

126. Nicholls, Robert J. (2004), "Coastal Flooding and Wetland loss in the 21st Century: Changes under the SRES climate and socioeconomic scenarios", ***Global Environmental change***, Vo.14, No.1: 69-86.

127. Church, J.A. et al. (2013), "Sea Level Change", in Stocker,T.F. et al. (eds.) ***Climate Change 2013: The Physical Science Basis.*** Contribution of Working Group I to the Fifth Assessment Report of the Intergovernmental Panel on Climate Change, Cambridge: Cambridge University Press, p.1140.

128. McGranahan, G. et al. (2007), "The rising tide: assessing the risks of climate change and human settlements in low elevation coastal Zones", ***Environment and***

million people dwell in the *Low Elevation Coastal Zone* (LECZ), that constitute 2% of the world's land mass.[129] In addition to this, the demography of coastal region has been expanding through the migration to this region. Furthermore, it is noted that in LECZ, 13% of the world's urban population resides in 65% of cities with population more than five million.[130]

The largest vulnerability of populations to coastal flooding from rise in sea level are estimated to be in South and in Southeast Asia, particularly India, Bangladesh, Pakistan, Eastern part of China, and southern part of Indonesia.[131] In addition, the foremost impact of climate change triggered rise in sea level will be higher on the low-lying coastal areas being susceptible to the risks of sea level rise and storms. In South Asia, these areas involve cities like Karachi, Mumbai, and Dhaka. These have experienced an important environmental crisis in recent years.[132]

Urbanization, Vol.19, No.17: 17-37; Smith, Anthony Oliver (2009), "Sea Level Rise and the Vulnerability of Coastal Peoples: Responding to the Local Challenges of Global Climate Change in the 21st Century", ***United Nations University-UNU-EHS-Institute for Environment and Human Security***, No.7/2009:1-52.

129. McGranahan, G. et al. (2007), "The rising tide: assessing the risks of climate change and human settlements in low elevation coastal Zones", ***Environment and Urbanization***, Vol.19, No.17: 17-37.

130. Ibid. 29; Smith, Anthony Oliver (2009), "Sea Level Rise and the Vulnerability of Coastal Peoples: Responding to the Local Challenges of Global Climate Change in the 21st Century", ***United Nations University-UNU-EHS-Institute for Environment and Human Security***, No.7/2009:20.

131. Hemming, D. et al. (2007), ***"Impacts of Mean Sea Level Rise Based on current state of the Art Modelling"***, Hadley Centre for Climate Prediction and Research, Exeter, UK.Quoted in Smith, Anthony Oliver (2009), "Sea Level Rise and the Vulnerability of Coastal Peoples: Responding to the Local Challenges of Global Climate Change in the 21st Century", ***United Nations University-UNU-EHS-Institute for Environment and Human Security***, No.7/2009:22.

132. Sivakumar, Mannava V.K. and Robert Stefanski, "Climate change in South Asia" Chapter 2, p.27, [Online: web] Accessed 17 July 2015 URL: file:///C:/Users/Prashant%20Kr.%20Sharma/Downloads/9789048195152-c2.pdf.

Research conducted by Dasgupta et al. (2007) observed that population would be at a huge loss due to the intense possibility of sea level rise in future. They estimated that susceptibility of population at one-meter sea level rise would engulf near about 56 million people, and that is supposed to engulf 89 million people at a two-meter rise and 245 million people for a rise of five-meter.[133] It has been observed that, in dearth of any other changes, 38 centimeters rise in a sea level would increase five-fold the number of people flooded by storm surges.[134]

The Bangladesh study predicts a 1 m rise in the level of sea by the middle of the next century. In addition, this increase in sea level is estimated to engulf about 5.608 million acres of present coastal land and this coastal land is about 15.8% of the total land area of Bangladesh. The areas, which will be inundated with sea level rise comprised of "65% of greater Khulna, 99% of Barisal, 100% of Patuakhali, 44% of Noakhali, and 12% of Faridpur."[135] The population will be affected severely due to sea level rise. It is estimated that "about 10 million of the country's 110 million population (2.05 million households) will be left with no option other than to migrate towards the safer place or say, affected urban cities like Dhaka, Chittagong, Khulna and Rajshahi."[136]

---

133. Dasgupta, S. eta al. (2007), "The impacts of Sea level rise on developing countries: a comparative analysis", World Bank Policy Research Working Papar, No. 4136, ***The World Bank,*** Washington DC, pp.9-10; Smith, Anthony Oliver (2009), "Sea Level Rise and the Vulnerability of Coastal Peoples: Responding to the Local Challenges of Global Climate Change in the 21st Century", ***United Nations University-UNU-EHS-Institute for Environment and Human Security***, No.7/2009:22.

134. Nicholls, Robert J. Et al. (1999), "Increasing flood risk and wetland losses due to global sea-level rise: regional global analyses", ***Global Environmental Change***, Vol. 9: 69-87; McGranahan, G. et al. (2007), "The rising tide: assessing the risks of climate change and human settlements in low elevation coastal Zones", ***Environment and Urbanization***, Vol.19, No.17: 17-37

135. "Greenhouse Effect and its Impact on the Region" a joint study undertaken under the declaration of the Fourth SAARC Summit (Islamabad, 29-31 December 1988) to provide a basis for a meaningful cooperation among member states, which completed in 1992, Chapter III, p.53, [Online: web] URL: http://www.saarc-sec.org/userfiles/Large%20Publications/RSGEIOR/index.php.

136. Ibid.53.

In addition, the mangrove forests of the Sundarbans will also get affected owing to sea level rise. It is believed that the mangrove forests of the Sundarbans will be ravaged gradually even before being flooded by possible sea level rise mainly because of slow increase in the level of salinity. Salinity ingression in Sundarbans has turned out to be a regular phenomenon. The Western portion of Sundarbans, where declining trends of fresh water are observed possibly owing to the diversion of substantial amount of water from the Farrakka Barrage, has resulted in an increase in the level of salinity. An increasing salinity in turn has reduced the regeneration process of an important plant species of Sundari.[137] With the larger frequency of storms and lower continental slopes, the eastern coast of India is more susceptible than the western coast to damages from storm surges.[138]

Chen observed that because of one-meter rise in the sea level, 40% of Chinese tidal-flat area (about 35,000 sq. km) will be below the sea level.[139] Mcfadden et al. (2007) in their research predicted a global loss of 33% and 44% of coastal wetlands (excluding sea grasses) given 36 cm and 72 cm rise in the level of sea from 2000 to 2080 respectively.[140]Trimble et al. (1998) have studied *the impacts of sea level rise on the regional water resources of Southern Florida* by using Florida water management model. They estimated that sea level rise of 15 cm will result into the greater water use cutbacks for the developed region and even the present rates of sea level will pose formidable challenges for regional water management in Southern Florida in the next few Decades.[141]

---

137. Ibid.62.

138. Ibid.73.

139. Chen, Junyong (1997), "The Impact of Sea Level Rise on China's Coastal Areas and Its Disaster Hazard Evaluation", ***Journal of Coastal Research,*** Vo.13, No.3, (Summer, 1997), p.927.

140. McFadden L, et al. (2007), "Broad-scale modeling of coastal wetlands: what is required?" ,***Hydrobiologia,*** 577: 5-15.

141. Trimble, P.J. (1998), "Preliminary Estimate of Impacts of Sea-Level Rise on the Regional Water Resources of Southern Florida", ***Journal of Coastal Research***, Special Issue, No.26. Proceedings of the Palm Beach International Coastal Symposium, 19-23 May (Spring 1998): 252-55.

Jogoo applied the concept of direct inundation or "drowning" to estimate land loss in Mauritius.[142] Ragoonaden observed that the main impact of sea-level rise for most of the coastal areas in Mauritius is land loss through submergence of lowland and loss of wetlands as well as erosion of beautiful sandy beaches that will have serious impact on country's economy in terms of tourism. In addition, the loss of territory due to sea level rise is projected to have 0.5% that constitutes the most valuable economic asset of the island, which is a major source of recreation and main attraction of the tourist industry.[143]

The next section discusses the laws and policies undertaken by India and Bangladesh to address the growing concern of environment and climate change.

2.3. Legal Regime in the Realm of Environmental Protection in India and Bangladesh

Both India and Bangladesh have been the innocent victims of the climate change induced several susceptibilities like extreme weather events, changes in temperature and precipitation patterns, sea level rise, affecting all aspects of human being. However, India and Bangladesh remained determined to tackle these tribulations. Both countries have taken initiatives to overcome the environmental problems.

2.3.1. Legal Regime in India

The constitution of India provides for the protection of environment. Article 21 of the Indian Constitution stipulates the right to life as a fundamental right of its citizens. Moreover, this provision of right

142. Jogoo, V. (1992), ***"Assessing the Impacts-Mauritius Case Study"***, Presented at the International workshop, The Rising challenge of the Sea, Margarita, Venezuela March 1992.

143. Ragoonaden, Sachooda (1997), "Impact of Sea Level Rise on Mauritius", ***Journal of Coastal Research, Special Issue,*** No.24, Island States At Risk: Global Climate Change, Development and Population (Fall 1997): 205-223.

to life has been delineated broadly by the Indian Judiciary to include also, amongst others, right to livelihood, right to clean environment and right to live with dignity. In addition to this, under the directive principles of state policy, states are entrusted with protecting and improving the environment and the forests and wildlife. It is also the fundamental duty of every citizen of India to protect and improve the national environment encompassing forests, lakes, rivers, and wildlife, and to have compassion for living creatures. Furthermore, the Indian constitution entrusts the local bodies comprising elected representatives with the onus to protect and safeguard the local environmental capital stock.[144]

India has launched an elaborate set of policies with regard to the conservation and governance of the environment. Its strategy for addressing the environmental and climate change problems is reflected in many of its social and economic development programmes. The major policy legislations set out to overcome the problems in India are as follows:

Indian Forest Act, 1927

The Indian Forest Act of 1927 stipulates legal framework for management of forests in the country. This Act is applicable in some states as it is, while some of the states have enacted their own laws that in essence, are the adopted and modified version of the Indian Forest Act 1927.[145]

144. Mahadevia, Kanksha and Mayank Vikash, "Climate change-Impact on the Sunderbans: A case Study", ***International Scientific Journal Environmental Science,*** p.11. [Online: web] Accessed 7 July 2015 URL: http://environment.scientific-journal.com/articles/2/1.pdf.

145. Ministry of Environment, Forest and Climate Change, Government of India, "Introduction", [Online: web] Accessed on 1 July 2015 URL: http://envfor.nic.in/division/introduction-10.

The Environment (Protection) Act, 1986

This Act was enacted in 1986 with the purpose of providing for the protection and improvement of the environment. It allows the Central Government to set up authorities [under section 3(3)] charged with the mandate of preventing all forms of environmental pollution and to tackle specific environmental problems, which are peculiar to different parts of the country. In 1991, this Act was last amended.[146]

National Environment Policy (NEP) 2006

The National Environment Policy launched in 2006, which outlines the essential elements of India's response to climate change. It seeks to enhance the coverage, and fill in the lacunae that still exist, in the light of current knowledge and accumulated experience. This legislation is intended as a guide, which is based on the principle of sustainable development. Some of its prime objective is to protect and conserve the critical ecological systems and resources, to ensure equitable access to environmental resources and quality for all sections of society, to ensure the judicious use of environmental resources to meet the requirements and aspirations of the present and future generations of our society. Further, this legislation sets out to integrate environmental concern into policies, plans, programmes, and projects for economic and social development.[147]

National Green Tribunal Act (NGT), 2010

The National Green Tribunal (NGT), 2010 is a specialized body that is equipped with the necessary expertise to deal environmental disputes involving multi-disciplinary issues. This act came into effect on 18th October, 2010 for the effective and expeditious disposal of

146. Ministry of Environment, Forest and Climate Change, Government of India, "Environment Protection", [Online:web] Accessed 1 July 2015 URL: http://envfor.nic.in/division/environment-protection.

147. Ministry of Environment & Forests, Government of India, Annual Report 2012-13, p. 342.

cases pertaining to the environmental protection and conservation of forests and other natural resources encompassing enforcement of any legal right concerning to environment and providing relief and compensation for damages to persons and property and for matters connected therewith or incidental thereto. This tribunal is not bound by the procedure stipulated under the Code of Civil Procedure, 1908, but is guided by the principles of natural justice.

The dedicated jurisdiction of Tribunal in environmental affairs shall provide speedy environmental justice and help reduce the litigation burden in the higher courts. Five zonal benches have been notified i.e. New Delhi, Pune, Kolkata, Bhopal and Chennai. The benches at New Delhi and Chennai have been operationalized. In addition to the Chairperson, three judicial and nine expert members staff this tribunal.[148]

National Environment Assessment and Monitoring Authority (NEAMA)

The Ministry of Environment, Forest and Climate Change, under the Environment (Protection) Act, 1986 has proposed to set up a National Environment Assessment and Monitoring Authority (NEAMA) in order to strengthen and professionalize the regimes of environmental impact assessment and coastal zone management. This monitoring authority would include area expertise, technological finesse and field outreach and its constitution shall be a part of larger regulatory reforms exercise to improve environmental regulation.[149]

National Forest Policy, 1988

The Government of India redrafted the National Forest Policy in 1988 in order to improve the consideration of the issues of the

---

148. Ministry of Environment & Forests, Government of India, Annual Report 2012-13, p. 342.

149. Ibid.342.

environmental sustainability, conservation, and social and economic values of forests. In addition, this policy stipulates that derivation of direct economic benefit must be subordinated to its principal aim. This policy subsequently led to the establishment of the Joint Forest Management Resolution of the 1990. Following this policy shift the Government of West Bengal had issued two specific guidelines in 1991 and 1996 for the management of the Sundarbans. These are Mangrove Forest areas of the Sundarbans; and National Parks and Sanctuaries of the State respectively.[150]

Biodiversity Act, 2002[151]

This Act has been passed with an intention to conserve and protect biodiversity and sustainable use of its components.

National Biodiversity Action Plan, 2008

The National Biodiversity Action Plan was rolled out in 2008 primarily to consolidate and augment existing strategies and programmes pertaining to biodiversity. It identifies the ravaging impact of the climate change on biodiversity and proposes several points for the action to be taken to mitigate this. This action required inclusion of research into this area and policymaking. In 1999, the National Policy and Macro-level-Action Strategy on Biodiversity was developed with the same above-mentioned purpose to consolidate and enhance the then existing strategies and programmes relating to biodiversity. One of the primary methods of conservation of biodiversity in India has been through according the special status and protection to biodiversity rich areas by declaring them as national parks, wildlife sanctuaries, biosphere reserves, and ecologically fragile and sensitive areas.[152]

---

150. Danda, Anamitra Anurag and Gayathri Srikanthan (2011), "Indian Sundarbans Delta: A Vision", ***WWF Policy Document India.***

151. Sonak, Dr. Sangeeta et al., "Review of Marine and Coastal Policies in India", ***The Energy and Resources Institute***, Western Regional Centre, Goa: Teri.

152. Mahadevia, Kanksha and Mayank Vikash, "Climate change-Impact on the

National Forestry Action Programme (NFAP)

This programme is a comprehensive strategic long-term plan that is supposed to be made for the next 20 years in order to address major issues related to the forestry sector in line with the National Forest Policy, 1988. The main objective of this programme is to bring one-third area of the country under forest /tree cover and to cease the activities of deforestation in order to achieve sustainable development of forests.[153]

National Forest Commission[154]

The National Forest Commission has been established by the resolution dated February 7th, 2003 by the Ministry of Environment and Forests. This Commission has been established to review the working of the Forests and Wildlife Sector.

The National Action Plan on Climate Change (NAPCC)[155]

The National Action Plan on Climate Change has been a major step in realm of climate change policy to address the growing concern of climate change. This plan is coordinated by the Ministry of Environment and Forest. Furthermore, it is implemented through the various nodal ministries in specific areas or sectors. The Prime

---

Sunderbans: A case Study", ***International Scientific Journal Environmental Science,*** p.11. [Online: web] Accesssed 7 July 2015 URL: http://environment.scientific-journal.com/articles/2/1.pdf.

153. Ministry of Environment, Forest and Climate Change, Government of India, "Introduction", [Online: web] Accessed 1 July 2015 URL: http://envfor.nic.in/division/introduction-10.

154. Ministry of Environment, Forest and Climate Change, Government of India, "Introduction", [Online: web] Accessed 1 July 2015 URL: http://envfor.nic.in/division/introduction-10; Ministry of Environment and Forest, Government of India (2003), "Working Paper", [Online: web] Accessed 10 July 2015 URL: http://www.moef.nic.in/sites/default/files/nfc-wpaper.pdf.

155. Ministry of Environment & Forests, Government of India, Annual Report 2012-13, pp. 350-52.

Minister, Dr. Manmohan Singh, released India's first NAPCC on 30th June, 2008. This plan outlines the existing and future policies and programmes to address the climate mitigation and adaptation. This plan discerns eight-core "national mission" viz. National Solar Mission, National Mission for Enhanced Energy Efficiency, National Mission on Sustainable Habitat, National Water Mission, National Mission for Sustaining the Himalayan Ecosystem, National Mission for a "Green India", National Mission for Sustainable Agriculture, National Mission on Strategic Knowledge for Climate Change. This plan has emphasized the priority of maintaining high economic growth rates to uplift the living standards. In addition, the plan "identifies measures that promote development objectives while also yielding co-benefits for addressing climate change effectively."

The NAPCC also delineates other ongoing initiatives, encompassing Power Generation, Renewable Energy, and Energy Efficiency. The Prime Minister's Council on Climate Change has approved all national missions. In line with the initiative of the Central Government on climate change, State Governments are also preparing the State Action Plans on Climate Change, which aims at building institutional capacities and implementing sectoral activities to address climate change. As of now, to address the climate change concern 21 states of India have prepared their charts on State Action Plan on Climate Change (SAPCC). These States are Andaman and Nicobar, Andhra Pradesh, Arunachal Pradesh, Assam, Delhi, Jammu & Kashmir, Kerala, Karnataka, Lakshadweep, Madhya Pradesh, Manipur, Meghalaya, Mizoram, Nagaland, Odisha, Punjab, Rajasthan, Sikkim, Tripura, Uttarakhand, and West Bengal.

Parliamentary Forum on Global Warming and Climate Change

The speaker of Lok Sabha, in consultation with the Chairman, Rajya Sabha constituted this forum on 14thJuly, 2008. The functions of this forum include the following:

1. To identify problems relating to the Global Warming and Climate Change and make necessary suggestions and recommendation for the government or organizations concerned to reduce the extent of climate change;
2. To discern the various ways to involve Members of Parliament to have interactions with the specialist of National and International Bodies working on Global Warming and Climate Change to develop new technologies to mitigate Global Warming;
3. To organize seminars and workshop to bring awareness among the Members of Parliament about the causes and effects of Global Warming and Climate Change;
4. To take appropriate such related major as it may deem fit.

In short, India's broad environmental legislative framework consists of "Environmental Protection Act, 1986; the Water (Prevention and Control of Pollution) Act, 1974; the Air (Prevention and Control of Pollution) Act, 1981; the Indian Wild Life (Protection) Act, 1972 (Amended in 1983, 1986, 1991,1997, 2001); the Biodiversity Act, 2002; Coastal Regulation Zone Notification, 1991; Forest (Conservation) Act, 1980; Hazardous Waste Management Act, 1989; Environmental Impact Assessment Notification, 1994; Indian Fisheries Act, 1987; Deep Sea Fishing Policy 1991; Marine Fisheries Regulation Acts; Indian Ports Act, 1908, Major Port Trust Act, 1963; Merchant Shipping Act, 1958, Coast Guard Act, 1978, Maritime Act; National Environmental Tribunal Act, 1995."[156]

Moreover, "India has also been a signatory to number of multilateral environmental agreements and conventions, encompassing the UN Framework Convention on Climate Change (UNFCCC), Kyoto Protocol, and Convention on Biological Diversity (CBD). Apart from this, India is also party to some of the related conventions, namely the

156. Sonak, Dr. Sangeeta et al., "Review of Marine and Coastal Policies in India", ***The Energy and Resources Institute***, Western Regional Centre, Goa: Teri.

Convention on International Trade in Endangered Species of Wild Flora and Fauna, the Ramsar Convention on Wetlands of International Importance, and the Convention on Migratory Species."[157]

2.3.2. Legal Regime in Bangladesh

Bangladesh has enacted and implemented a number of laws and policies to grapple the environmental problems from time to time. The environmental laws that exist in Bangladesh deal specifically with the subjects of land use, air, and water pollution, noise, toxic elements, solid waste, wildlife protection, forest conservation, mineral resources and coastal zone management, environmental health and sanitation, and other related issues.[158]

Some of the important laws,[159] which are now in force, are as follows:

1. The Forest Act (1927), which was inherited from pre-independence times. In addition to this, some of the laws were enacted between 1947 and 1971, and some laws came after 1971;
2. Environment Pollution Control Ordinance (1977), which is the primary law on the environment in Bangladesh deals with the air, water, and soil pollution;
3. The Town Improvement Act (1953) and the Factories Act (1965), both these laws have provisions pertaining to the

157. Mahadevia, Kanksha and Mayank Vikash, "Climate change-Impact on the Sunderbans: A case Study", ***International Scientific Journal Environmental Science,*** [Online: web] Accessed 7 July 2015 URL: http://environment.scientific-journal.com/articles/2/1.pdf.

158. "Greenhouse Effect and its Impact on the Region" a joint study undertaken under the declaration of the Fourth SAARC Summit (Islamabad, 29-31 December 1988) to provide a basis for a meaningful cooperation among member states, which completed in 1992, Chapter IV, p.85 [Online: web] URL: http://www.saarc-sec.org/userfiles/Large%20Publications/RSGEIOR/index.php.

159. Ibid.85-86.

protection of the workers' health and sufficient sanitation measures in factories. The Factories Act also empowers the chief Inspector of Factories to manage the use and disposal of toxic and all other pollutants;

4. Moreover, the Pesticides Ordinance (1971), the Bengal Motor Vehicle Act (1939), the Motor Vehicle Rules (1940) modified in 1980, Bangladesh Penal Code (1960);
5. Bangladesh Environmental Preservation Ordinance;

The Government of Bangladesh has launched the following steps to tackle climate change in Bangladesh.

1. **National Adaptation Program of Action (NAPA)**[160]

   The Government of Bangladesh along with the other least developed countries has prepared its NAPA in 2005 to address adaptation activities immediately and urgently. The NAPA of Bangladesh consists of 15 priority projects to be implemented with the assistance from the Least Developed Countries Fund (LDCF) came to an existence under the United Nations Framework Convention on Climate Change. Under the NAPA-community based coastal afforestation program – the first priority adaptation activity, which is presently being implemented by the Department of Forests at a cost of US$4 million.

2. **Climate Change Cell at the Department of Environment**[161]

   In 2004, under the overarching Disaster Management Program, the Government of Bangladesh (GOB) with the support of the Department for International Development (DFID, UK), has established a Climate Change Cell (CCC) at the Department

---

160. Chowdhury, Junayed Ahmed (2012), "Public Participation in Bangladesh's Response to Climate Change Issues", ***Advocates for International Development.***

161. Ibid.

of Environment to augment the capacity of the GOB to better coordinate and facilitate climate change activities.

3. **Climate Change Trust Fund**[162]

   The GOB has allotted US$96 million approximately under the banner of climate change Trust Fund.

4. **Bangladesh Climate Change Strategy and Action Plan (BCCSAP)** 2009[163]

   This plan controls those programme focusing on six strategies areas: food security, social protection and health; comprehensive disaster management; infrastructure; research and Knowledge management; mitigation and low carbon development; capacity building and institutional strengthening.

In addition to this, Bangladesh is a signatory to a number of multilateral forums. Bangladesh became party to UNFCCC on June 9, 1992 and ratified it on April 15, 1994. It came into force on 5 January 1999. Bangladesh ratified Kyoto Protocol on 22 October 2001 and entered into force on 16 February 2005.[164]

162. Ibid.

163. "Climate Change Laws of Bangladesh" Sabin Center for Climate Change Law, Columbia Law School, [Online: web] Accessed 1 August 2015 URL: http://web.law.columbia.edu/climate-change/resources/climate-change-laws-world/bangladesh.

164.. Ibid.

Chapter Three

The Sundarbans: Understanding its Ecological and Socio-Economic Features

The Sundarbans is the world's largest single contiguous block of mangrove ecosystem criss-crossed by the maze of tidal rivers extending across the Southern portion of India and Bangladesh. The floral and faunal diversity of this ecosystem makes it unique around the world. The natural resources of this forest are one of the major sources of livelihoods for the inhabitants of the Sundarbans especially Mawali, Bawali and fisher-folks. Its environmental protective roles aside, the resources generated from the forestland contribute to both the rural and national economy of the country. Bangladeshi Government is a significant beneficiary of it.

This chapter is categorized into two sections. Firstly, ecological profile where focus has been given on etymology, physiography (including origin of the Sundarbans), geography, ecosystem, environment and biodiversity; and secondly, socio-economic profile in which focus has been on history and cultural values, demography, social structure and political economy of the Sundarbans.

3.1. Ecological Profile

3.1.1. Etymology

The name Sundarbans literally translates as "beautiful forest" in the Bengali language (*Shundor,* "Beautiful" and *Bon,* "Forest" or "Jungle"). It is said so that the Sundarbans may have been derived from the

Sundari Trees (*Heriterra Fomes*) that was found in the Sundarbans in large numbers.[165] Furthermore, pertaining to the nomenclature of the Sundarbans, two other opinions also exist. Some opine that the Sundarbans is situated facing towards the sea, so the name had been derived from the Samudraban which means "forest within the sea."[166] After the twist of the word, the forest later modified as the "Sundarbans." Another opinion divulges that the name of the forest is Sundarbans because it is in fact a beautiful forest.[167]

3.1.2. Physiography

The origin of the Sundarbans is perhaps baffling and mysterious mainly because of its crisscrossed riverine basin.

The gradual deposition of alluvial silt brought from the folded Himalayas through centuries resulted in the basic formation of this lower Gangetic delta.[168] Morgan and Mc Intire observed that the tract of the Sundarbans has fallen under the Ganga delta that is very dynamic, and the formation of delta is very rapid here. This process resulted in an unequal thickness and width of the surface horizon, but it is found that the "morphological nature"[169] of the whole Sundarbans is more or less uniform.[170]

165. Bhattacharjee, Tapaleena T. et al. (2011), "The Sinking "Beauty"- Sunderbans", ***Geospatial World Forum.***

166. Mandal, R.N. et al. (2010)," Dwindling Indian Sunderban Mangrove: The Way out", ***Science and Culture***, 76(7-8): 275-282.

167. Ibid.275.

168. Choudhury, Biswajit Roy and Pradeep Vyas (2005), ***"The Sunderbans"***, New Delhi: Rupa Pubication India Pvt. Ltd. p.10.

169. The term "morphological" pertains to the geological structure i.e. geomorphological features of the Black Hils", structural effects of folding and faulting of surface of the earth (Internet source). This is used in the context of the tract of Sundarbans where delta formation is not a new phenomenon. The Gangetic delta is a very dynamic and ever changes its position. The changes in the morphological nature of Sundarbans always becomes apparent due to the active delta region.

170. Morgan, J.P. and McIntire, W.G. (1959), "Quarternary Geology of the Bengal Basin, East Pakistan and Burma" ***Bull. Geol. Soc. Am.,*** 70:319-42.

Chowdhury and Vyas while noting the views of the geologist and structuralist Oldham, state that the entire tract of the Sundarbans is a delta, formed solely by the drainage of the mighty rivers of the Gangetic plain.[171] Oldham also suggested that the trough of the land was caused by the presence of a mammoth alluvial deposit that pushed the earth's crust down. It is considered as mysterious and confusing in that some study observes the stretches of this tract goes up to the plateau of Chotanagpur (Jharkhand) and Kolkata (West Bengal).[172] This is partly corroborated by the fact that some fossils of an estuarine nature were found while digging a deep-well near Garden Reach, Kolkata, at a depth of 950ft.[173] Some observations by pollen analytical study and study of the peat soil claimed that the present metropolis of Kolkata was under the mangrove swamps of Sundarbans 5000 years back.[174]

Chowdhury and Vyas cited the view of another geologist J. Fargusson who stated that the entire basin of Bengal was shallow land in the early Pleistocene age;[175] and in the late Pleistocene age, sea retreated outright from this area, and the raft of alluvial deposits brought by the

---

171. Choudhury, Biswajit Roy and Pradeep Vyas (2005), ***"The Sunderbans"***, New Delhi: Rupa Pubication India Pvt. Ltd. p.10.

172. Ibid.10.

173. Ibid.10.

174. Ghosh, A.K. (1941), "Submerged Forests in Calcutta", Sci. & Cult., 6: 669-70. Chanda, S. and Mukherjee, B.B. (1969), "Radio Carbon Dating of Two Microfosiliferous Quaternary Deposites in and around Calcutta, ***Sci. & Cult.***, 35: 275-6. Mukherjee, S. K. (1969), "Survey of Plants Resources of India and its Use", ***Bull. Bot. Surv. India***, 11 (3&4): 217-23. Mukherjee, B. B. (1972), "Quaternary Pollen Analysis as a Possible Indicator of PrehistoricAgriculture in the Deltaic Part of West Bengal, ***J. Palynol.***, 8: 144-51. Vishnu Mitre and H.P. Gupta (1972), "Pollen Analysis Study of Quaternary Deposits in the Bengal Basin", ***Paleobotanist***, 19: 297-306.Sen, P. and M. Banerjee (1984), "On the occurrence of Reptilian Remmants in the Peat Bed of Barrackpore, 24-Parganas, West Bengal, ***Paleobot. Soc. Ind.***, 29: 47-51. Quoted in Naskar, Kumudranjan and D. N. Guha Bakshi (1987), ***Mangrove Swamps of the Sundarbans: an Ecological Perspective***, Calcutta: Naya Prokash, p. 9.

175. "Pleistocene Age" is categorically regarded as the time period, which started about 1.8 million years ago and that lasted until about 11,700 years ago. (Source- Google).

rivers shrouded the marine sediments.[176] Deb mentioned that the area of Sundarbans is quite recent in origin and comprised only the alluvial plain of lower Bengal. This was formed by the deposition of sediments raising 6m-9m above mean sea level, due to the water erosion from the Himalaya. The oceanic tidal sediments further assisted this.[177] Allison et al. (2003) mentioned that today's delta of Ganges-Brahmaputra-Meghna came to an existence between 2500 and 5000 years ago by the silt formation carried by the river Ganges.[178] Some scientists have studied the physiography of the Sundarbans regions in relation to tidal action. They argue that the silt rushed back from the Bay of Bengal due to the tidal wave and the presence of innumerable tidal estuaries; it was pushed back into the moribund channels that led to rising of the riverbed. The blocked water resulted into the formation of an island.[179]

Hence, we find that there are diverse views on the history of evolution of Sundarbans tract. However, excavations, assumptions and theories explain that, the process of delta formation due to simultaneous upheavals and subsidence still carries on.

3.1.3. Geography

The Sundarbans is situated in the vast delta of Bay of Bengal shaped by the convergence of the Ganges, Brahmaputra and Meghna rivers across southern part of India and Bangladesh.[180] It stretches over the districts of 24 Parganas of West Bengal, Khulna, Backergunge and Sathkhira

176. Choudhury, Biswajit Roy and Pradeep Vyas (2005), ***"The Sunderbans"***, New Delhi: Rupa Pubication India Pvt. Ltd. p.10.

177. Deb, S. C. (1956), "Paleoclimatology and Geophysics of the Ganga Delta", ***Geographical Review of Inda***, 28: 11-18.

178. Alison et al. (2003), "Stratigraphic evolution of the late Holocene Ganges-Brahmputra lower delta planning sedimentary", ***Sedimentary Geology***, 155 (3-4):317-342.

179. Choudhury, Biswajit Roy and Pradeep Vyas (2005), ***"The Sunderbans"***, New Delhi: Rupa Pubication India Pvt. Ltd. p.11.

180. Bhattacharjee, Tapaleena T. et al. (2011), "The Sinking "Beauty"- Sunderbans", ***Geospatial World Forum***.

of Bangladesh.[181] The administrative boundary of Indian part of Sundarbans is spread over two districts of West Bengal i.e. South 24 Parganas and North 24 Parganas. The Sundarbans fall a bit south to the tropic of cancer.[182] The Indian Sundarbans exists between the latitude 21°32' to 22°40'N and longitude 88°03' to 89°E.[183]

The Bangladeshi part of Sundarbans lies between the latitude 21°30' to 22°30' N and longitude 89°12' to 90°18'E.[184] The boundaries of the Indian Sundarbans extend over the area from the river Hooghly in the west to the Ichamati-Raimangal (Herobhanga or Harinbari River) in the east,[185] and Dampier-Hodges line drawn in 1829-1830 in the north to the Bay of Bengal in the south.[186] The Bangladeshi Sundarbans consists of three wildlife sanctuaries: Sundarbans West, East and South[187] and is bounded in north by Bagerhat, Khulna and Sathkhira districts, in south by Bay of Bengal, in the east by Baleswar

181. Naskar, Kumudranjan and D. N. Guha Bakshi (1987), ***Mangrove Swamps of the Sundarbans: an Ecological Perspective,*** Calcutta: Naya Prokash, p.6. Rahman, M R and M Asaduzzaman (2010), "Ecology of Sunderban, Bangladesh", ***J.Sci, Foundation,*** 8(1&2): 37.

182. Naskar, Kumudranjan and D. N. Guha Bakshi (1987), ***Mangrove Swamps of the Sundarbans: an Ecological Perspective,*** Calcutta: Naya Prokash, p.6.

183. Choudhury, Biswajit Roy and Pradeep Vyas (2005), ***"The Sunderbans"***, New Delhi: Rupa Pubication India Pvt. Ltd. p.115.

184. Amin, Muhammad Nurul and Niaz Ahmed Khan (2001), "A Primer on the Nature and Management of the Sunderbans", ***Grassroots Voice: A Journal OF Indigenous Knowledge and Development***, Vol.VI, issue: 1, p.87. Rahman, M R and M Asaduzzaman (2010), "Ecology of Sunderban, Bangladesh", ***J.Sci, Foundation,*** 8(1&2): 37.

185. Naskar, Kumudranjan and D. N. Guha Bakshi (1987), ***Mangrove Swamps of the Sundarbans: an Ecological Perspective,*** Calcutta: Naya Prokash, p.6. Danda, Anamitra Anurag and Gayathri Srikanthan (2011), "Indian Sundarbans Delta: A Vision", ***WWF Policy Document India,*** p.4.

186. Dipanjan Ghosh and Sreeparna Ghosh (2013), "Sunderban Mangroves: Challenges to Survival", ***Feature Article***: 44. Danda, Anamitra Anurag and Gayathri Srikanthan (2011), "Indian Sundarbans Delta: A Vision", ***WWF Policy Document India,*** p.4.

187. Rahman, M R and M Asaduzzaman (2010), "Ecology of Sunderban, Bangladesh", ***J.Sci. Foundation,*** 8(1&2): 37.

(or Haringhata) river, Perojpur and Barisal districts, and in the west by Raimangal and Harinbhaga rivers which partially form the boundary with India.[188]

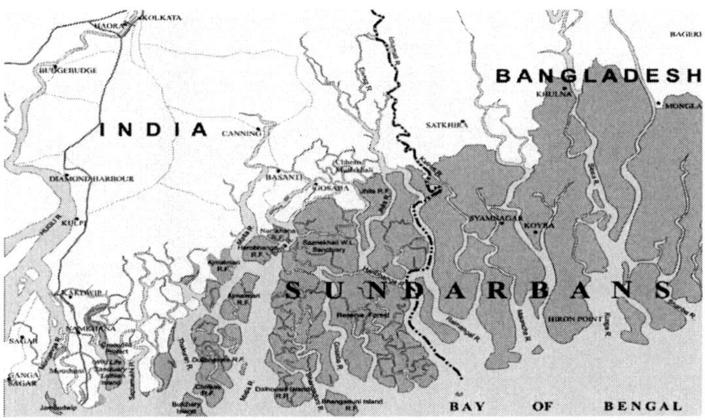

Map: 3.1. The Sundarbans region stretching on both side of the border
Source- URL:https://easyvivek.files.wordpress.com/2011/06/sundarban-map.jpg

Extending through India to Bangladesh, it covers an area of about 26,000 square km that forms the largest single stretch of mangrove vegetation.[189]They further stated that two-thirds of the Sundarbans lies in Bangladesh; and Indian Sundarbans covers an area of about 9630 square km; out of which the reserve forest occupies near about 4263 square km; and South 24 Parganas Forest Division holds 1660 sq. km.[190] The Sundarbans located in Bangladesh occupies 60% of mangrove forest areas and remaining 40% rests with India.[191] The Bangladeshi

188. Amin, Muhammad Nurul and Niaz Ahmed Khan (2001), "A Primer on the Nature and Management of the Sunderbans", ***Grassroots Voice: A Journal OF Indigenous Knowledge and Development***, Vol.VI, issue: 1, p.87.

189. Choudhury, Biswajit Roy and Pradeep Vyas (2005), ***"The Sunderbans"***, New Delhi: Rupa Pubication India Pvt.Ltd, p.8.

190. Ibid.115.

191. Rahman, M R and M Asaduzzaman (2010), "Ecology of Sunderban, Bangladesh", ***J.Sci. Foundation,*** 8(1&2): 35;Dipanjan Ghosh and Sreeparna Ghosh (2013), "Sunderban Mangroves: Challenges to Survival", ***Feature Article***: 44.

part of Sundarbans accounts for 4.2% of country's total land area and holds 40% of the Bangladesh's total forest tracts.[192] Moreover, this forest tract covers only 10.2% of the land area of Bangladesh.[193]

Map: 3.2. Indian Sundarbans

Source- URL: https://tripsntours.files.wordpress.com/2015/02/map-of-sundarban.jpg

3.1.4. The Riverine System

The Sundarbans, located in Lower Bengal – the land of rivers, is intersected by an elaborate maze of rivers, channels and creeks with varying width and length. The Indian Sundarbans is also known as the Hooghly (the lower part of Ganges) – Matla estuary. It is the place where fresh water of the rivers mingles with the Bay of Bengal and the seawater ingresses into hundreds of creeks and channels during the high tide.[194] The vast rivers of the Hooghly-Raimangal estuary in West Bengal are either the tributaries of the Ganga and /or the outcomes of the funnel shaped Bay of Bengal.[195]

---

192. Haq, Syed Azizul (2010), "Impact of climate change on Sunderbans", a paper presented in 18th Commonwealth Forestry Conference 2010 on 28 June- 02 July 2010 at Edinburg International Conference Center, Scotland, UK, p.2.

193. Ibid.2.

194. Choudhury, Biswajit Roy and Pradeep Vyas (2005), ***"The Sunderbans"***, New Delhi: Rupa Pubication India Pvt.Ltd, p.12.

195. Naskar, Kumudranjan and D. N. Guha Bakshi (1987), ***Mangrove Swamps of the Sundarbans: an Ecological Perspective,*** Calcutta: Naya Prokash, p.10.

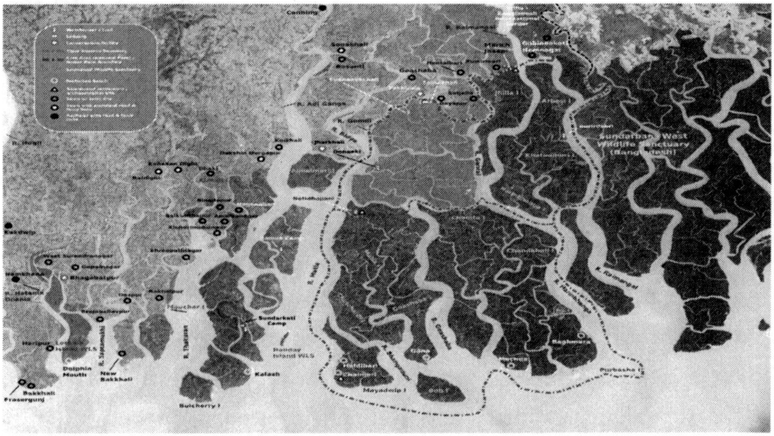

Map: 3.3. Showing river systems of the Sundarbans
Source- URL: https://upload.wikimedia.org/wikipedia/commons/5/57/Sundarbans_map.png.

The rivers of the Indian part of Sundarbans do not carry much silt and freshwater in comparison to those of the Bangladeshi Sundarbans. As a result, these rivers receive more seawater inside.[196] Naskar and Bakshi also substantiated it and stated that the rivers of the western and southwestern portions are normally more saline than the eastern side.[197] The salinity is intense in Indian Sundarbans and varies from as low as eight parts per thousand to as high as twenty parts per thousand (PPT).[198] The rivers like Ichhamati, Kalindi, Harinbari/Herobhanga and Gosaba get fresh water from the upper reaches. These rivers also receive fresh water from the Padma river of Bangladesh.[199] On the other hand, due to a massive flow of water from the river Hooghly to

---

196. Choudhury, Biswajit Roy and Pradeep Vyas (2005), *"The Sunderbans"*, New Delhi: Rupa Pubication India Pvt.Ltd, p.13.

197. Naskar, Kumudranjan and D. N. Guha Bakshi (1987), ***Mangrove Swamps of the Sundarbans: an Ecological Perspective,*** Calcutta: Naya Prokash, p.10.

198. Choudhury, Biswajit Roy and Pradeep Vyas (2005), *"The Sunderbans"*, New Delhi: Rupa Pubication India Pvt.Ltd, p.14.

199. Naskar, Kumudranjan and D. N. Guha Bakshi (1987), ***Mangrove Swamps of the Sundarbans: an Ecological Perspective,*** Calcutta: Naya Prokash, p.10.

the river Padma, the freshwater rivers like Matla and Bidyadhari do not get much freshwater and have almost changed up to tidal rivers. The huge ingression of seawater in the rivers of Indian Sundarbans looks like outstretched arms of the sea rather than freshwater rivers.[200]

Rahman and Asaduzzaman have classified the river system of Bangladeshi Sundarbans in three different series based upon the manner in which the tidal wave propagates through the major river system, i.e., Raimangal-Sibsa series, Passur-Sibsa series and Passur-Baleswar series. Moreover, they also stated that from east to west the river system comprises four estuaries, i.e., Bangra estuary, Kungna estuary, Malancha estuary and Raimangal estuary.[201] The important rivers of the Indian Sundarbans are Matla, Bidyadhari, Saptamukhi, Thakuran, Gosaba, Raimangal, and Ichhamati.[202]

Three rivers, Bidyadhari, Khuratya and Rampura Khal, join near canning and flow as a wide- mouthed Matla into the Bay of Bengal. Bidyadhari is a branch of Hooghly. Saptamukhi originates near Sultanpur and traverses 80 km to merge into the sea. Thakuran originates from Joynagar and with the name of 'Jamira' enters in to the Bay of Bengal. Many canals of the Raimangal and Matla meet together and form the river Gosaba. Raimangal originates from Sahebkhali and is joined by many rivers like Terobank and Harinbhaga on its way to the sea. Ichhamati derives its origin from Churni. It flows towards south supplying freshwater to the Gosaba and Raimangal.[203]

---

200. Choudhury, Biswajit Roy and Pradeep Vyas (2005), ***"The Sunderbans"***, New Delhi: Rupa Pubication India Pvt.Ltd, p.14.

201. Rahman, M R and M Asaduzzaman (2010), "Ecology of Sunderban, Bangladesh", ***J.Sci. Foundation,*** 8(1&2): 38.

202. Choudhury, Biswajit Roy and Pradeep Vyas (2005), ***"The Sunderbans"***, New Delhi: Rupa Pubication India Pvt.Ltd, p.14.

203. Naskar, Kumudranjan and D. N. Guha Bakshi (1987), ***Mangrove Swamps of the Sundarbans: an Ecological Perspective,*** Calcutta: Naya Prokash, pp.11-12. Choudhury, Biswajit Roy and Pradeep Vyas (2005), ***"The Sunderbans"***, New Delhi: Rupa Pubication India Pvt.Ltd, p.14.

3.1.5. Soils of the Sundarbans

The entire coastal strip of India encompassing the delta of the Sundarbans retains mostly saline soil. In the Sundarbans delta, the saline soil strip stretches about 50 km from the Bay engulfing the low-lying islands, estuaries and the islands.[204] Dipanjan Ghosh and Sreeparna Ghosh have stated that the active delta of the Sundarbans contains various types of soil such as silty clay fertile soil, sandy clay, soil with organic and peaty deposits, swampy and marshy soil (also known as 'mangrove soil').[205] The saline soils of the Sundarbans are regarded as the factor responsible for the higher plant mortality[206] and salinity of the surface soil is governed by the quantity of freshwater flow and monsoonal rainfall.[207] The salinity goes up to maximum level in the middle of the May (summer) and lowers when monsoon starts.[208]

The surface soil is clay and loam in the eastern part of the Bangladeshi side of Sundarbans, whereas it is harder and less suitable for the growth of tree in the west.[209] In most part of the Sundarbans, the soil salinity remains between 5.2 to 16 micromhos (mmhos)/cm in May-April during the dry season and in rainy time 0.65 to 8.97

---

204. Yadav, J.S.P. et al. (1979), "Coastal Saline Soils of India", ***CSSRI Bull,*** No.5, pp.6-34.

205. Dipanjan Ghosh and Sreeparna Ghosh (2013), "Sunderban Mangroves: Challenges to Survival", ***Feature Article***: 44.

206. Naskar, Kumudranjan and D. N. Guha Bakshi (1987), ***Mangrove Swamps of the Sundarbans: an Ecological Perspective,*** Calcutta: Naya Prokash, p.16.

207. Dipanjan Ghosh and Sreeparna Ghosh (2013), "Sunderban Mangroves: Challenges to Survival", ***Feature Article***: 44.

208. Naskar, Kumudranjan and D. N. Guha Bakshi (1987), ***Mangrove Swamps of the Sundarbans: an Ecological Perspective,*** Calcutta: Naya Prokash, p.16.

209. Chowdhury, A.M. (1968), ***Working plan of the Sunderban forest Division for the period from 1960-61 to 1979-80,*** Vol. I, Government of East Pakistan, Forest Department, Dacca: 82. Quoted in Amin, Muhammad Nurul and Niaz Ahmed Khan (2001), "A Primer on the Nature and Management of the Sunderbans", ***Grassroots Voice: A Journal OF Indigenous Knowledge and Development,*** Vol.VI, issue: 1, p.88.

mmhos/cm.[210] The soil pH is more or less acidic and alkaline that ranges from 5.4 to 7.8.[211] Nevertheless, soil contains adequate water, but owing to the high concentration of salts mostly chloride, sulphate and bicarbonate sodium salts, magnesium and calcium plants can not avail of the water.[212]

3.1.6. Water of the Sundarbans

The water of the Sundarbans is mainly saline with electrical conductivities ranges from 10-40 mmhos/cm. With this saline water, agricultural activities are largely impossible. This increasing trend of salinity is caused by the frequent intrusion of seawater. This intrusion completely inundates or deluges most of the riverine terrain and mud flat lands during the high tides.[213] The only agricultural water that is supplied here is during the monsoonal rain or flashings.[214]

"In the delta of Indian Sundarbans three types of aquifer zones are found: the first is shallower one that is found within 60m below ground level (bgl). This is mainly brackish. The second zone, which is even brackish in nature, is found between 70-160m bgl; and the final

---

210. Rahman, M R and M Asaduzzaman (2010), "Ecology of Sunderban, Bangladesh", *J.Sci. Foundation,* 8(1&2)*:* 38.

211. Naskar, Kumudranjan and D. N. Guha Bakshi (1987), ***Mangrove Swamps of the Sundarbans: an Ecological Perspective,*** Calcutta: Naya Prokash, p.16; Dipanjan Ghosh and Sreeparna Ghosh (2013), "Sunderban Mangroves: Challenges to Survival", ***Feature Article***: 44.

212. Dipanjan Ghosh and Sreeparna Ghosh (2013), "Sunderban Mangroves: Challenges to Survival", ***Feature Article***: 44.

213. Naskar, K.R. and Guha Bakshi, D.N. (1982), Sunderbans-the world famous Mangrove forest of the District 24- Parganas in West Bengal, ***J.Econ.Tax. Botany***, 3: 883-918; Naskar, Kumudranjan and D. N. Guha Bakshi (1987), ***Mangrove Swamps of the Sundarbans: an Ecological Perspective,*** Calcutta: Naya Prokash, p.20.

214. Naskar, K.R. (1981), ***Floristic Studies of the District 24-Parganas in West Bengal (India) with special Reference to the Mangrove vegetation of the Sundarbans,*** Ph.D Thesis, University of Calcutta; Naskar, Kumudranjan and D. N. Guha Bakshi (1987), ***Mangrove Swamps of the Sundarbans: an Ecological Perspective,*** Calcutta: Naya Prokash, p.20.

aquifers zone is of fresh nature i.e. sweet water. This zone is observed 160m to 400m bgl. The saline water aquifers that exist at top are divided by the underlying group of freshwater aquifers by a thick clay layer ranging in thickness from 4m at Gangasagar to 120m at Kultali, and the general thickness of the intervening clay blanket is observed between 20-50m."[215]

Yadav et al. (1981) illustrated that underground water table is shallow and enriched with high salt contents; and the salt molecules during the dry season is observed moving along with water to the surface soil by capillary action.[216] With the evaporation of the surface water, the molecules of salt remain on the surface soil, which is accumulated in toxic amount for plant growth.[217] This is perhaps the reason that only the mangrove species can survive well on this soil.[218]

3.1.7. Climatic Conditions of the Sundarbans

Naskar and Bakshi stated that the existence of large scale network of creeks, rivers and the proximity of the Bay of Bengal help in modulating the extreme climate. Hence, the extreme climatic conditions do not prevail in the Sundarbans. They further mentioned that a day is moderately warm, equitable and humid and night temperatures

215. Sinha Ray, S.P. (2010), "Status of Ground water condition in Sunderbans area, West Bengal Commissioned Report. Quoted in Danda, Anamitra Anurag and Gayathri Srikanthan (2011), "Indian Sundarbans Delta: A Vision", ***WWF Policy Document India.***

216. Yadav, J.S.P. et al. (1981), "Management of coastal Saline Soils of Sunderbans", ***Bull 7 (CSSRI-ICAR)***, Karnal, India, pp.1-32; Naskar, Kumudranjan and D. N. Guha Bakshi (1987), ***Mangrove Swamps of the Sundarbans: an Ecological Perspective,*** Calcutta: Naya Prokash, p.20.

217. Chattopadhyay, G.N. et al. (1983), A note on the Possibilities of Salinization of soils under Paddy-cum-brackishwater Aquaculture in Coastal Saline Soils, ***J. Indian Soc.Coastal agric. Res.,*** 1(1):43-45.

218. Naskar, K.R. (1983), Halophytes and their Unique Adaptation on the Sundarbans Mangrove Swamps in India, ***J. Indian Soc. Coastal agric. Res,*** 1(2):91-105; Naskar, Kumudranjan and D. N. Guha Bakshi (1987), ***Mangrove Swamps of the Sundarbans: an Ecological Perspective,*** Calcutta: Naya Prokash, p.20.

increase slowly. The cold weather prevails from November to February, and rainfall is negligible during this period.[219] WWF India Report (2011) has pointed out that the climate of this region is tropical with high relative humidity between 70-88%; the mean maximum temperatures during June is 34°C, and mean minimum temperature is 11°C during January. Furthermore, this report stated that barring January and February, the region experiences occasional rains through most of the year. The monsoon period accounts for about 80% of the annual precipitation, which happens mostly between June and October.[220]

Every year 4-5 cyclonic storms are common in lower delta of Ganga. WWF India Report (2011) considers that the Indian Sundarbans delta is prone to extreme weather events, which are frequent in the pre-monsoon period.[221]Bose states that the cyclones exhibit an increase in intensity and frequency of occurrence.[222] These cyclones occur with tidal surge and autumnal storm.[223]

3.1.8. Floristic Compositions of the Sundarbans

The floral diversity of Sundarbans is very impressive and euphonious than any other mangroves in the world. Patil depicted that Sundarbans retains half of the total number of mangrove species observed in the world.[224] Blasco et al. (2001) mentioned that mangroves, covering less

219. Naskar, Kumudranjan and D. N. Guha Bakshi (1987), ***Mangrove Swamps of the Sundarbans: an Ecological Perspective,*** Calcutta: Naya Prokash, p.21.

220. Danda, Anamitra Anurag and Gayathri Srikanthan (2011), "Indian Sundarbans Delta: A Vision", ***WWF Policy Document India.***

221. Ibid.

222. Bose, Sahana, "Human Influence on Mangrove Ecosystem in Indian Sunderbans: An Earth Atmospheric Interaction", Jawaharlal Nehru University, New Delhi.

223. Rahman, M R and M Asaduzzaman (2010), "Ecology of Sunderban, Bangladesh", ***J.Sci. Foundation,*** 8(1&2)***:*** 38.

224. Patil, R.P. (1962), "Our Mangrove Resources", Trop. Ecol.3, ½, 70-1. Quoted in Rashid, S.Harun.et al. (2008), "Undergrowth Species diversity of Sunderban mangrove Forest (Bangladesh) in relation to Salinity", ***Ber.Inst.Landschefts-PFlanzenokologic Uni. Hohenheim Heft***: 43.

than 3% of the world's tropical forests (about 180,000 sq.km.) and consisting of a limited number of woody species (about 70 species of trees and shrubs across the world's tropic), play an imperative role for the coastal population and their countries especially in Asia.[225] There are many definitions of what constitutes a mangrove and what the floristic compositions of the Sundarbans are.

The term 'mangroves' is derived from Portuguese and English words i.e. 'Mangue' and 'grove,' respectively. In Portuguese, a mangrove tree or bush is called 'Mangue', while the community of mangrove trees and bushes are 'mangal.'[226] Chowdhury and Vyas have defined mangroves as trees of various species and several families, which can grow, survive, and propagate in seawater or swampy brackish water and alluvial soil in a tidal zone. For that reason, the mangroves are found largely at the edges of tropical seas, bays, lagoons and estuarine regions.[227] Blasco et al. (1975) defined mangrove as the name given to a particular type of coastal woody vegetation that fringes muddy saline shores and estuaries in tropical and subtropical regions and much of the ground is covered by the seawater at high tide.[228] Naskar and Guha have defined mangroves as the formation of coastal tropical forest that is encircled or spread by the tidal rivers and /or the seawater, and are inundated frequently by the tidal water.[229]

---

225. Blasco, F. et al. (2001), "Depletion of the mangroves of Continental Asia", ***Wetlands Ecology and Management,*** 9:245.

226. Naskar, Kumudranjan and D. N. Guha Bakshi (1987), ***Mangrove Swamps of the Sundarbans: an Ecological Perspective,*** Calcutta: Naya Prokash, p.31.

227. Choudhury, Biswajit Roy and Pradeep Vyas (2005), ***"The Sunderbans"***, New Delhi: Rupa Pubication India Pvt.Ltd, p.16.

228. Blasco, F. (1975), ***The Mangroves in India*** (translated by Mrs. K.Thanikaimoni from LES MANGROVES DE L'INDE), Institute Francais de Pondichery, Inde, Sri Aurobinda Abraham, Pondicherry, India. Quoted in Naskar, Kumudranjan and D. N. Guha Bakshi (1987), ***Mangrove Swamps of the Sundarbans: an Ecological Perspective,*** Calcutta: Naya Prokash, p.32.

229. in Naskar, Kumudranjan and D. N. Guha Bakshi (1987), ***Mangrove Swamps of the Sundarbans: an Ecological Perspective,*** Calcutta: Naya Prokash, p.31.

Generally, mangroves are apparent along the coastlines of tropical and sub-tropical regions. It is usually found between 25°N and 25°S latitude across the world. However, there is some exception to these statements. Mangroves are also found as far south as New Zealand and as far north as Japan.[230] Asia occupies 46% of most of the world's mangroves, followed by America with 35% and Africa with 17%.[231] In national standpoint, Indian Sundarbans mangrove occupies 62% area about 2,400 Sq.km. maintaining 90% species diversity followed by Andaman and Nicobar Island with 76.5% and Bhitarkanika, Orissa with 72.3% with regard to existing major mangrove diversity.[232] In global perspective, both the Old World tropics and the New World tropics, (consisting of 40 true mangrove and 8 true mangroves respectively), constitute 48 true mangrove species together.[233]

It is reported that the Indian Sundarbans contains 70% of all the species of the world's mangrove;[234] and 84 species of flora have been discerned here;[235] of which 34 belong to the true mangroves and rest of the varieties pertain to the mangrove associated and back mangrove

---

230. Choudhury, J. K. (1997), ***Sustainable management of coastal mangrove***, Forest development and social needs, XI World Forestry Congress, Antalya, Turkey. Rashid, S. Harun. et al. (2008), "Undergrowth Species diversity of Sunderban mangrove Forest (Bangladesh) in relation to Salinity", ***Ber.Inst.Landschefts-PFlanzenokologic Uni. Hohenheim Heft***: 41-56.

231. Rashid, S. Harun. et al. (2008), "Undergrowth Species diversity of Sunderban mangrove Forest (Bangladesh) in relation to Salinity", ***Ber.Inst.Landschefts-PFlanzenokologic Uni. Hohenheim Heft***: 42.

232. Mandal, R.N. et al. (2010)," Dwindling Indian Sunderban Mangrove: The Way out", ***Science and Culture***, 76(7-8): 277.

233. Tomlinson, P.B. (1986), ***The Botany of Mangrove***, Cambridge: Cambridge University Press. Quoted in Mandal, R.N. et al. (2010)," Dwindling Indian Sunderban Mangrove: The Way out", ***Science and Culture***, 76(7-8): 277.

234. Choudhury, Biswajit Roy and Pradeep Vyas (2005), ***"The Sunderbans"***, New Delhi: Rupa Pubication India Pvt. Ltd.

235. Ibid; Dipanjan Ghosh and Sreeparna Ghosh (2013), "Sunderban Mangroves: Challenges to Survival", ***Feature Article***: 45.

species.[236] Heining had recorded 69 species of mangroves comprising 34 families in the entire Sundarbans of India and Bangladesh.[237] On the other hand, Mandal et al. (2009) have shown that Indian Sundarbans constitutes 69 intertidal plant species; of which 30 species belong to true mangrove, 20 species mangrove associates and 12 species back mangrove.[238] The more recent study holds up the view that the area of Sundarbans may contain about 140 mangroves, mangrove associates, back mangrove and coastal zone flora.[239] Kathiresan and Rajendran stated that the Indian Sundarbans delta accounts for 85% of all mangrove habitats found in India. They further mentioned that 63 out of 69 mangrove plant species observed in India exist in the ISD.[240]

In Indian Sundarbans, the mangrove forest remained restricted to the inter-tidal belts at the interface of the land-sea. Mangroves encounter to the high and low tides twice in a day. The roots of the mangrove trees are modified so that they could stand firmly in the mud. Some trees like Keora (*Sonneratia apetala*) have evolved the aerial roots that obtrude out of the mud upwards like spikes owing to the dearth of oxygen. These roots are known as 'pneumatophores' and commonly called respiratory roots which ensure the appropriate supply of oxygen to the deeper roots.[241]

---

236. Choudhury, Biswajit Roy and Pradeep Vyas (2005), ***"The Sunderbans"***, New Delhi: Rupa Pubication India Pvt. Ltd.

237. Heining, R.L. (1892), ***Working plan of Sundarbans government forest,*** Khulna and 24-Parganas district, Bengal, Calcutta, Bengal Secretariat Press.

238. Mandal, R.N. et al. (2010)," Dwindling Indian Sunderban Mangrove: The Way out", ***Science and Culture***, 76(7-8): 277.

239. Naskar, K. R. and A.P. Sharma (2010). Coastal zone vegetation in India with reference to mangroves and need for their conservation. Quoted in ***Sundarbans issues and threats***, Central Inland Fisheries Research Institute and West Bengal Biodiversity Board. Quoted in Danda, Anamitra Anurag and Gayathri Srikanthan (2011), "Indian Sundarbans Delta: A Vision", ***WWF Policy Document India.***

240. Kathiresan, K. and N. Rajendran (2005). Grow mangroves for protecting coral reefs. ***SDMRI Research Publication,*** 9: 41-48.

241. Choudhury, Biswajit Roy and Pradeep Vyas (2005), ***"The Sunderbans"***, New Delhi: Rupa Pubication India Pvt. Ltd.

Given the wide range of plant species belonging to assorted families, mangroves flowering plants can be classified generally into three types of floral components; viz. true mangroves, back mangroves and mangrove associates.[242] Further, this mangrove forest can again be subdivided in to two kinds, viz. i) Swampy mangrove[243] that stands below the high tide and inundates twice a day by sea water and ii) Tidal mangrove[244] that deluges only during the period of spring tide and cyclones or by exceptional tide.

Figure: 3.1. The Sundarbans Mangrove
Source-URL: http://www.shunya.net/Pictures/NorthIndia/Sunderbans/Sunderbans38.jpg.

The true mangrove species are salt tolerant halophytic plants that grow on tidal swampy habitats. These kinds of species develop in high salinity, regular tidal inundation, oxygen deficient fine clay soil, fresh water flow and heavy wind as well. Such kinds of species are Jatbaen (*Avicennia officinalis*), Pairabaen (*A.alba*), Kalabaen *(A. marina)*, Garia

242. Dipanjan Ghosh and Sreeparna Ghosh (2013), "Sunderban Mangroves: Challenges to Survival", ***Feature Article***: 45.

243. Aubreville 1970; Blasco 1975. Quoted in Naskar, Kumudranjan and D. N. Guha Bakshi (1987), ***Mangrove Swamps of the Sundarbans: an Ecological Perspective,*** Calcutta: Naya Prokash, p.32.

244. Qureshi, I.M. (1959), "Botanical, Silvicultural features of Mangroves forests of Bombay state", ***Proc. Mangrove Symposium***, Faridabad, India, pp.20-26.

(*Kandelia candel*), Kripa (*Lumnitzera racemosa*), and Tora (*Aegialitis rotundifolia*), etc. These mangroves possess pneumatophores to ensure appropriate intake of oxygen for the deeper roots as it is discussed above. The species of back mangrove are bushy and discontinuous types of plant. These mangroves do not experience the situation the true mangrove species do. Nevertheless, these species are able to withstand high salinity and nutrient deficient soil at the edges of coast, it is found largely towards landward tracts. Such species are Garjan *(Rhizophora apiculata)*, Goran (*Ceriops decandra*), Mathgoran *(C. tagal*), Bakul (*Bruguiera cylindrical*), and Keora (*Sonneratia apelata*).The mangrove associates species are not true mangrove plants; but rather these are the mesophytic plants that grow adjacent to the human habitation. These species include Gewa *(Excoecaria agallocha*), Kankra (*Bruguiera gymnorrhiza*), Khalsi (*Aegiceras corniculatum*), Ora (*Sonneratia caseolaris*) and Hental (*Phoenix paludosa*).[245]

In addition to this, there are some mangrove species that are rare and confined to certain specific salinity zone. These are Amur (*Agalia domestica*), Passur (*X. mekongensis*), Dhundul (*Xylocarpus granatum*), Sundari (*Heritera Fomes*) and Golpata (*Nypa fructicans*). The trees like Sundari and Golpata are of highly specific commercial importance, and are rarely sighted.

Rahman and Asaduzzaman[246] elucidate that the highest freshwater flows are restricted to the Bangladeshi Sundarbans. Owing to this, the level of salinity is much less than the Indian side of Sundarbans. That is

245. Rashid, S. Harun. et al. (2008), "Undergrowth Species diversity of Sunderban mangrove Forest (Bangladesh) in relation to Salinity", ***Ber.Inst.Landschefts-PFlanzenokologic Uni. Hohenheim Heft***: 41-56. Naskar, Kumudranjan and D. N. Guha Bakshi (1987), ***Mangrove Swamps of the Sundarbans: an Ecological Perspective,*** Calcutta: Naya Prokash, pp.33-35. Rahman, M R and M Asaduzzaman (2010), "Ecology of Sunderban, Bangladesh", ***J.Sci, Foundation,*** 8(1&2): 35-47. Dipanjan Ghosh and Sreeparna Ghosh (2013), "Sunderban Mangroves: Challenges to Survival", ***Feature Article***: 44-48.

246. Rahman, M R and M Asaduzzaman (2010), "Ecology of Sunderban, Bangladesh", ***J.Sci, Foundation,*** 8(1&2): 35-47.

why in Bangladeshi Sundarbans a large number of populations of less salt tolerant or freshwater loving species of mangrove exist such as *Heritera Fomes* and *Nypa Fructicans*. Whereas in the Indian Sundarbans, low stands of Gewa (*Excoecaria agallocha),* Khalsi *(Agiceras Corniculatum)* and Goran *(Ceriops decandra)* are common. At the high salinity, mangroves spend more energy to maintain water balance. It is further reported that in Bangladeshi Sundarbans forest is dominated mostly by the presence of three major tree species, viz. *Heritera Fomes, Excoecaria agallocha* and *Ceriops decandra.*[247] Choudhury and Choudhury (1994) observed that seven species of the mangrove are endangered and needs immediate conservations efforts that are *Aegiceras Corniculatum, Heritera Fomes, Kandelia Kandel, Nypa Fructicans, Rhizophora spp., Sonneratia apetala* and *S. caseolaris.*[248]

Figure: 3.2. Goran Species in the Sundarbans
Source-URL: https://upload.wikimedia.org/wikipedia/commons/4/40/Sundarbans_02.jpg.

247. Rashid, S. Harun. et al. (2008), "Undergrowth Species diversity of Sunderban mangrove Forest (Bangladesh) in relation to Salinity", ***Ber.Inst.Landschefts-PFlanzenokologic Uni. Hohenheim Heft***: 41-56.

248. A. B. Choudhury, and A. Choudhury (1994), ***Mangroves of the Sunderbans***, Vol.1, India, IUCN, Bangkok.

Figure: 3.3. Sundari trees in the Sundarbans
Source-URL: http://mumbaigloss.in/wp-content/uploads/2013/07/Sundari-tree.jpg.

Figure: 3.4. Garjan trees in the Sundarbans
Source-URL: http://www.naturewildlife.org/sundarban.php?page=flora.

3.1.8.1. Significance of Mangroves

At least 30% of the land of any geographical tract is required to be under the forest cover for balancing the rainfall, regulating the temperature, high humidity and also to protect the tract from the natural hazards.[249] This forest functions as a bulwark against adverse circumstances.

249. Naskar, Kumudranjan and D. N. Guha Bakshi (1987), ***Mangrove Swamps of the Sundarbans: an Ecological Perspective,*** Calcutta: Naya Prokash, p.5.

Mangroves are of special significance for the Sundarbans; and act as the lifeline for the Sundarbans' sustainability.

De Groot et al. (2002) state that the ecosystem services of the mangrove forest of the Sundarbans have been categorized under four types: provisioning, cultural, regulatory, and supporting services.[250] The provisional services include the timber, fuel wood, fish, Nypa palm, honey-waxes, and medicinal plants. The cultural services include tourism, the status of a world heritage site, and the presence of religious places like Ganga Sagar and Hindu's abode of goddess. The regulatory services encompass the services like protection from cyclone, storm intensity, modulation of tidal deluge, assimilation of wastes, controlling soil erosion, nutrient cycling and carbon sequestration. Finally, the supporting services are to provide nurturing and nourishing ground to the various fish species, several wildlife animals and habitation for floral and faunal species.[251]

Naskar and Bakshi have also discerned two-fold role played by the mangrove forest of Sundarbans, viz. direct and indirect mainly to maintain the socio-economic life and eco-climatic stability of this tract. This mangrove forest in its indirect form plays the protective role and that is the most vital for its territorial existence. This protective role includes the conservation of soil and maintaining balance in nature. On the other hand, copious and prodigious economic value in its direct form encompasses sources of fuel, sources of timber and other

---

250. De Groot, R.S. et al. (2002), "A typology for the classification, description and Valuation of ecosystem functions, goods and services", ***Ecological Economics***, 41: 393-408.

251. Biswas, S.R. et al. (2007), "Do invasive plants threaten the Sunderbans mangrove forest of Bangladesh?" ***Forest Ecology and Management***, 245:1-9. Uddin, M.S. (2011***), Economic Valuation of Sunderbans mangrove ecosystem services- A case study in Bangladesh***, M.Sc. thesis, UNESCO-IHE, Netherlands. Uddin, Md. Shams, et al. (2013), "Climate Change on the Sunderbans Mangrove ecosystem services and dependent livelihoods in Bangladesh", ***Asian Journal of Conservation Biology,*** Vol.2, N.2, p. 152-156.

commercial articles, fodder, tannin, thatching leaves, wooden articles, honey, wax, alcoholic drink, medicine and other commercial goods.[252]

For instance, the woods of *Heriterra fomes* are good for the carpentry related work, boat building ends and also construction of buildings. Woods of this tree are durable, fine grained and strong. *Excoecaria agallocha* and *E. bicolor* woods are light and utilized in carpentry, building construction, making of fish boats, packing boxes and match splints. The trees of *Nypa fructicans* are useful and suitable for roofing the cottages of the area of the Sundarbans as these trees are strong. Honey obtained from the *Cynometra ramiflora* and *Aegiceras corniculatum* are of the best quality, and the species of *Ceriops decandra* generate bulk of good quantity of honey.[253]

In a nutshell, its significance can be illustrated as follows:

i. It produces substantial quantity of economically important material like timber, firewood, tannin, honey, wax and medicine.

ii. Mangroves act as a natural sewage treatment plants and it absorbs pollutants both from the air and water. Mangrove retains high quantity of tannins in its barks and leaves that can be helpful in neutralizing some of industrial effluents. It also acts as a carbon sink.[254] Keora is the most efficient species followed by the Baen and Gewa for carbon sink.

iii. The mangrove functions as a wind-breaking barrier, a natural buffer from damages by storms, surges, and minimizes the intensity of the extreme weather events.

iv. It acts as a breeding and feeding ground of shellfishes and fine-fishes.

---

252. Naskar, Kumudranjan and D. N. Guha Bakshi (1987), ***Mangrove Swamps of the Sundarbans: an Ecological Perspective,*** Calcutta: Naya Prokash. pp.198-209.

253. Ibid.

254. An ability to absorb carbon dioxide from the atmosphere by the forest, ocean or other natural environment is regarded as an act of carbon sink (Source- Google). The mangrove forest of Sundarbans is an important source of carbon absorption.

v. It generates leaf litter and debris, which fulfill the nutritional requirements of the young prawn, adult shrimps, mollusk and high economic valued fish.

vi. It is home to the single largest tiger population in the country.

3.1.9. Faunal Diversity of the Sundarbans

The ecosystem of the Sundarbans is unique, dynamic and more complex. The faunal species found in the Sundarbans are environmentally interacted in the process of ecosystem. The Sundarbans is only remaining habitats in the lower Bengal basin for a large number of various kinds of faunal species. In the Sundarbans, 49 mammal species have been documented.[255] The various kinds of presence of colourful bird-life to be seen along the waterways are one of the Sundarbans' magnificent attractions. From the Sundarbans, a total of 315 species of birds have been recorded.[256] Furthermore, nearly 53 species of reptile and 8 species of amphibians have been recorded.[257] Another source reported that in the forest habitats of the Sundarbans about 50 species of mammals, about 320 species of inland and migratory birds, about 50 species of reptiles, 8 species of amphibians, and about 400 species of fish exist.[258]

Given the vast diversity of faunal species in Sundarbans, this study only focuses on some important species of Sundarbans concisely. Due to the large extent of over exploitation of natural resources and increasing pollution, changing environment, the various species of

---

255. Amin, Muhammad Nurul and Niaz Ahmed Khan (2001), "A Primer on the Nature and Management of the Sundarbans", ***Grassroots Voice: A Journal OF Indigenous Knowledge and Development***, Vol.VI, issue: 1, pp.85-101.

256. Rahman, M R and M Asaduzzaman (2010), "Ecology of Sunderban, Bangladesh", ***J.Sci, Foundation,*** 8(1&2): 35-47.

257. Ibid.

258. "The Great Sundarbans (Bangladesh and India): Forest swamp, draw only border, UNESCO World Heritage Site', [Online: web] Accessed 24th January 2015 URL: http://wikimapia.org/1651148/The-Great-Sundarbans-Bangladesh-and-India.

this fragile ecosystem have also become vulnerable and are on the verge of extinction. Six species are now considered to be extirpated from the Indian part of Sundarbans, "namely: the water buffalo (*Bubalus bubalis*); the Swamp deer (*Cervus duvaucelli*); the Javan rhinoceros (*Rhinoceros sondaicus*); great Indian one-horned rhinoceros (*Rhinoceros unicornis*); the gharial (*Gavialis gangeticus*); and the chitra turtle (*Chitra indica*)."[259]Furthermore, it is reported that the barking deer is also locally extinct as it was last spotted in 1970.[260]

A list of faunal species is given below in Table 3.1 that illustrates the most important species of reptiles, birds, mammals that are ecologically sensitive. These species are classified as the critically endangered, vulnerable, and endangered and near threatened. Most of these species are also placed under the schedules of Indian Wildlife (Protection) Act, 1972, amended to date and/or IUCN Red Data Book. It is apparent that the most critically endangered species are namely: Leatherback Sea Turtle *(Dermochelys coriacea*), Hawksbill Sea Turtle (*Eretmochelys imbricata*), River Terrapin (*Batagur baska*), Red-crowned Roofed Turtle (*Batagur Kachuga*), and white-rumped Vulture (*Gyps bengalensis*). And the endangered species of Sundarbans are Three-Striped Roofed Turtle *(Batagur dhongoka*), Narrow-headed Softshell Turtle (*Chitra indica*), Asian Giant Softshell Turtle (*Pelochelys cantorii*), Greater Adjutant Stork *(Leptoptilos dubius*), Fishing cat (*Prionailurus viverrina*), Gangetic Dolphin (*Platanista gangetica)*, and Royal Bengal Tiger (*Panthera tigris tigris*).

---

259. Danda, Anamitra Anurag and Gayathri Srikanthan (2011), "Indian Sundarbans Delta: A Vision", ***WWF Policy Document India,*** p.9.

260. Ibid.9.

Table: 3.1 Threatened or Endangered Fauna of ISD

Groups/common name	Scientific name	IUCN Red List Status
	REPTILES	
1. Leatherback Sea Turtle	***Dermochelys coriacea***	Critically Endangered
2. Hawksbill Sea Turtle	***Eretmochelys imbricate***	Critically Endangered
3. Olive Ridley Sea Turtle	***Lepidochelys olivacea***	Vulnerable
4. River Terrapin	***Batagur baska***	Critically Endangered
5. Three-striped Roofed Turtle	***Batagur dhongoka***	Endangered
6. Red-crowned Roofed Turtle	***Batagur kachuga***	Critically Endangered
7. Spotted Pond Turtle	***Geoclemys hamiltonii***	Vulnerable
8. Crowned-River Turtle	***Hardella thurjii***	Vulnerable
9. Narrow-headed Softshell Turtle	***Chitra indica***	Endangered
10. Asian Giant Softshell Turtle	***Pelochelys cantorii***	Endangered
11. Indian Softshell Turtle	***Nilssonia gangetica***	Vulnerable
12. Indian Peacock Softshell Turtle	***Nilssonia hurum***	Vulnerable
13. Indian Rock Python	***Python morulus***	Near threatened
14. King Kobra	***Ophiophagus Hannah***	Vulnerable
	BIRDS	
1. White-rumped Vulture	***Gyps bengalensis***	Critically Endangered
2. Greater Adjutant Stork	***Leptoptilos dubius***	Endangered
3. Lesser Adjutant Stork	***Leptoptilos javanicus***	Vulnerable
4. Greater Spotted Eagle	***Aquila clanga***	Vulnerable
5. Darter	***Anhinga melanogaster***	Near Threatened
6. Black-headed Ibis	***Threskiornis melanocephalus***	Near Threatened
	MAMMALS	
1. Royal Bengal Tiger	***Panthera tigris tigris***	Endangered
2. Fishing Cat	***Prionailurus viverrina***	Endangered
3. Gangetic Dolphin	***Platanista gangetica***	Endangered

4. Irrawaddy Dolphin	***Orcaella brevirostris***	Vulnerable
5. Finless Porpoise	***Neophocaena phocaenoides***	Vulnerable

This table is taken from the WWF Policy document India (2011)

The Sundarbans is home to the largest number of tigers in India. According to the census of 2004, the number of tigers in the Indian Sundarbans was 274.[261] The population of tigers in Bangladeshi Sundarbans is reported to have 450 presently.[262] The "Status of Tigers in India, 2014" report stated that India now has 70% of the tiger population in the world. The latest assessment records 2,226 tigers, up 30% from the 1,706 in 2010.[263]Another finding states that the population of tigers in Indian Sundarbans has remained stable and is estimated to be 76.[264] This finding has become rather controversial as the state's Forest Department has come out with a different set of data i.e. at least 103 based on the images from the camera traps set up by the Wildlife Institute of India (WII) and the World Wildlife Fund for Nature (WWF), in India.[265] The WII and WWF have recorded the number at 100 in 2004.[266] The assessment at the national level was based on the '*state of the art technology*' which meant that there was very little extrapolation based on data.[267]

---

261. Choudhury, Biswajit Roy and Pradeep Vyas (2005), ***"The Sunderbans"***, New Delhi: Rupa Pubication India Pvt.Ltd.

262. Rahman, M R and M Asaduzzaman (2010), "Ecology of Sunderban, Bangladesh", ***J.Sci, Foundation,*** 8(1&2)*:* 35-47.

263. Menon, Meena (2015), "Tiger Census Good News from The Jungle: Giant leap for big Cat", ***The Hindu***, Delhi, 21 January 2015.

264. Singh, Shiv Sahay (2015), "Report underestimates tiger count in Sunderbans", ***The Hindu***, Delhi, 23 January 2015.

265. Ibid.

266. Ibid.

267. Menon, Meena (2015), "Tiger Census Good News from The Jungle: Giant leap for big Cat", ***The Hindu***, Delhi, 21 January 2015.

3.2. Socio-Economic Profile

This section deals with socio-economic profile in which focus has been on history and cultural values, demography, social structure and political economy of the Sundarbans.

3.2.1. History and Cultural Values[268]

Owing to the changing course of rivers, cyclones and floods, which always affected the land formation of this Sundarbans area, accurate information of its earliest history of human habitation is not easily available. Archeological evidences do indicate that there has been human habitation in the Sundarbans from around 300 B.C. to 1200 A.D. However, perpetual onslaughts of the pirates, natural calamities, and erosive activities razed the entire human population from this tract. Christensen stated that due to the pirate attacks human population ceased to exist.[269]

The Sundarbans tract was for the first time surveyed by the Mughal emperor Akbar's appointee Minister of Revenue (Diwan-i-Ashraf) Todar Mall in 1582 in order to settle the revenue of the land between Hijli of Midnapore district and the plains of the south-east. This location was earlier known as 'Bhati'. After that, Suja, son of the emperor Shahjahan conducted a new survey in 1652. He termed the region as Muradkhana and Jitratkhana. He classified the Sundarbans tract into various parganas or revenue divisions that was Nimakmahal, Jangalmahal, Batia, Balanda, Sarfarjpur, Amirabad, Paihati, Madanamalla, Sagar etc. When the concept of district came to light,

268. This section is largely taken from the writing of the Biswajit Roy Chowdhury and Pradeep Das (2005). Choudhury, Biswajit Roy and Pradeep Vyas (2005), ***"The Sunderbans"***, New Delhi: Rupa Pubication India Pvt. Ltd.

269. Christensen, B. (1984), ***Ecological Aspects of the Sundarbans***, FO: TC P/BGD/2309 (mf), FAO, Rome, p.42. Quoted in Amin, Muhammad Nurul and Niaz Ahmed Khan (2001), "A Primer on the Nature and Management of the Sundarbans", ***Grassroots Voice: A Journal OF Indigenous Knowledge and Development***, Vol.VI, issue: 1, pp.85-101.

the district of lower Bengal was formed by assimilating all these 24 revenue division and is currently known as 24 parganas. Futhermore, these 24 parganas is divided into two separate districts that are South and North 24 Parganas.

During 1760s, the Sundarbans emerged as an essential business hub for forest produces like timber, honey, paraffin, salt and fish. From that period onward, the exploitation of natural resources began in the true sense of the term. The 24 Parganas was handed over to the East India Company following trounce of Nawab in the battle of Plassey in 1756. Moreover, the land was leased to individuals by the company to reclaim land for the cultivation and supply of timber in 1770. The lease of land was for the first three year at free of rent and after which 2 annas per *bigha* was charged. However, due to lack of fresh water, execrable and erratic weather conditions, and unsuitability of land for cultivation led the people to migrate from that area. However, Zamindars and land-holders lured the helpless people of some benefit from nearby places to settle in the Sundarbans. Moreover, the construction of embankment of around 2200 miles to prevent the cyclone and seawater at the edges of bay also spurred the people to settle there.

The cultural bondage between the people of Sundarbans is so strong that it reflects in their religious harmony. As both (Hindus and Muslim) religious communities worship the same God with different name. For instance, *'Bonobibi'* is considered as the goddess of the forest who is deified everywhere in Sundarbans and the term *'Bonobibi'* is perhaps akin to the Hindu goddess of *'Bonodevi.'* During the Muslim ruling, the former became more acceptable. *'Dakshin Rai'* is worshipped as the tiger-god under the banyan tree, *peepal* or *neem*. Equivalent to it, *'Pir'* and *'Gazi Saheb'* were discerned as the tiger god. The Goddess *'Manasa'* was worshipped to gratify the venomous snake. And *'Jagatgouri'* was deified for the cobra snake, *'Manik Pir'* for Welfare of cows, *'Olabibi'* for the prevention of cholera, *'Satyanarayan* or *Satyapeer'* for general welfare of the folks etc. In addition to this, the sailors pray for the best of everything to '*Badar Peer'* and five other *'Peers'* before sailing.

Moreover, many inherent cultural practices are performed. For instance, '*Bhado*' is solemnized as the rainy season festival; '*Tusu*' is observed as the winter festival. '*Karmopujo*' is also a popular tribal gesture festival. Even the WWF India (2011) mentions that in the Indian Sundarbans the caste and religious identities are not a strong determining factor in availing any opportunities offered through the Government.

3.2.2. Demography

The populations what are seen today in the Sundarbans are descendants of settlers who had arrived here during the colonial administration. Hence, two types of categories can be observed among the past settlers of the Sundarbans: one is of those who came to look for new opportunities as the frontiers were being opened up; and the others were those who arrived to escape the oppression in their place of origin. Furthermore, another tiny group of tribal from Chotanagpur plateau is also found. This group was brought to clear the forest and has remained on the margins of society. Population in the Indian Sundarbans has remained balanced between two prime religion of this tract Hinduism and Islam; and has co-existed peacefully and in harmony for generations.[270]

In the Indian Sundarbans, out of 108 islands, 54 are inhabited and population is around 4.4 million according to 2011 census,[271]whereas

---

270. Danda, Anamitra Anurag and Gayathri Srikanthan (2011), "Indian Sundarbans Delta: A Vision", ***WWF Policy Document India,*** pp.11-13.

271. The World Bank (2014), ***Building Resilience for Sustainable Development of the Sundarbans: Strategy Report,*** JS Print O Pack: New Delhi.

Bangladeshi Sundarbans consists of about 200 islands[272] with a population spread of around 7.5 million.[273]

3.2.3. Social Structure and Political Economy of the Sundarbans

The Sundarbans (in both part of India and Bangladesh) performs an important role in the acceleration of rural and national economy respectively. The people of the Sundarbans are totally dependent on the natural resources for their sustenance. The Sundarbans provides the patterns of livelihoods based mainly on fisheries, honey collection, wood and golpata collection. However, the practices of agriculture are the main stay of economy in the Indian part of Sundarbans. The rain fed agriculture being the main stay of economy at the Indian side is made possible with the construction of earthen embankment to keep the brackish tidal water at the edges of Bay.[274] Over 88.5% of the population exclusively depends on the pattern of livelihood that grows only during the rainy season with mono-cropped paddy cultivation.[275] This could be the cause of so much of poverty among the population inhabiting in the Indian Sundarbans. Chowdhury and Vyas estimated around 94% of the inhabitants depending upon the agriculture. Owing to the lack of freshwater and increased salinity level, the other means of agriculture is not suitable.[276]Though, some of the known salt tolerant

272. "The Great Sunderbans (Bangladesh and India): Forest swamp, draw only border, UNESCO World Heritage Site', [Online: web] Accessed 24th January 2015 URL: http://wikimapia.org/1651148/The-Great-Sundarbans-Bangladesh-and-India.

273. WWF Report India (2010), "Sundarbans: Future Imperfect: Climate Adaptation Report".

274. Danda, Anamitra Anurag and Gayathri Srikanthan (2011), "Indian Sundarbans Delta: A Vision", ***WWF Policy Document India,*** pp.11-13.

275. Naskar, Kumudranjan and D. N. Guha Bakshi (1987), ***Mangrove Swamps of the Sundarbans: an Ecological Perspective,*** Calcutta: Naya Prokash.

276. Choudhury, Biswajit Roy and Pradeep Vyas (2005), ***"The Sunderbans"***, New Delhi: Rupa Pubication India Pvt. Ltd.

paddy varieties could be cultivated such as Matla and Hamilton, these practices have eroded sharply on the wake of Green Revolution.[277]

Fishing is another source of livelihoods for the Sundarbans. The landless rural poor people work as daily wage earners in the aquaculture farm; and chronic poverty-stricken people are also dependent upon collection of prawn seed to earn quick cash that leads to the loss of fish biodiversity.[278] In the coastal zone of Bangladesh, fishing being an important source of income and employment largely contributes to the livelihoods of the poor fishers. This zone also accounts for 40% of total pond-fish production and 36% of inland capture fisheries.[279] Sundarbans holds around 172 species of fish, 20 species of prawn and 44 species of crabs.

Forestry is another significant source of occupation and subsistence for the people of Sundarbans. The forest resources include timber, wood for paper pulp, plywood, and barks for tannin, honey, wax and golpata.[280] It is estimated that about one million people rely on its resources for their livings and livelihoods.[281] Over 5 to 6 lakh people such as Mowali (Honey collectors), Bawalis (Wood and Golpata collectors), and Jeles (Fisherman)[282] are directly dependent on

277. Danda, Anamitra Anurag and Gayathri Srikanthan (2011), "Indian Sundarbans Delta: A Vision", ***WWF Policy Document India,*** pp.11.

278. Kumar, Pushpam (2012), "Impact of economic drivers on mangroves of Indian Sunderbans: an exploration of missing links", ***Environ Dev Sustain*** 14: 952.

279. Sarkar, Khalekuzzaman (2013), "Fisher Livelihoods in the Sunderbans". [Online: web] URL: ewcbookstore.org/fox/foxRuralLivelihoods005-ch04.pdf (2014).

280. Choudhury, Biswajit Roy and Pradeep Vyas (2005), ***"The Sunderbans"***, New Delhi: Rupa Pubication India Pvt. Ltd.

281. Sohela, Mustari (2013), "The Challenges and Coping Strategies of 'Mowal' the Honey collectors of Sunderban, Bangladesh", ***International Research Journal of Social Sciences***, vol.2 (6) 7-11.

282. Chandra, Ganesh and R. L. Sagar, "Fisheries in Sunderbans: Problems and Prospects", [Online: web] Accessed 24th January 2015 URL: http://ssrn.com/abstract=2084014.

the forest resources of the Sundarbans.[283] The forest resources generate good amount of revenue (Taka 15 to 16 crore every year) for the government of Bangladesh.[284]

Honey collection, the most unsafe (the attacks of tigers, snake and crocodile, forest robbers and other difficulties) are common to them[285] and tricky job performed by the Mowalis risking their life intruding deep into the forest,[286] is the most profitable one and is treated as the liquid gold.[287] The Mowalis are one of the indigenous[288] and traditional honey collectors in the reserve forest of Sundarbans representing the poorest sections of society.[289] The honey collection season starts from March-April and continues for about two or three months.[290] Sohela mentions that the suitable month for collection of honey is the three months of the year from Bangla 18th Chaitra to 18th Jaistha.[291] In 2013, the Forest department of the Eastern Division of Khulna had fixed

---

283. Special Correspondent (2014), "6 lakh working people in Sunderbans need hospital", [online: web] Accessed 24th January 2015 URL: http://thedailynewnation.com/news/8090/6-lakh-working-people-in-sundarbans-need-hospital.html.

284. Ibid.

285. Ray, Dr. Tapan (2013), "Traditional Honey Collecting: Emerging Livelihoods Problems And Socio-economic uplift of Mawalis Community in Sunderbans", Department of Bengali, Karimganj College, Karimganj, Assam, India, Vol.II, Issue II.

286. Kaizer, Fahad (2014), "A day with 'Mowals-The hunters of golden liquid", [online:web] Accessed 24th January 2015 URL: http://www.dhakacourier.com.bd/a-day-with-%E2%80%98mawals%E2%80%99-%E2%80%93-the-hunters-of-golden-liquid/.

287. Ibid.

288. Sohela, Mustari (2013), "The Challenges and Coping Strategies of 'Mowal' the Honey collectors of Sunderban, Bangladesh", ***International Research Journal of Social Sciences***, vol.2 (6) 7-11.

289. Kaizer, Fahad (2014), "A day with 'Mowals-The hunters of golden liquid", [online:web] Accessed 24th January 2015 URL: http://www.dhakacourier.com.bd/a-day-with-%E2%80%98mawals%E2%80%99-%E2%80%93-the-hunters-of-golden-liquid/.

290. Choudhury, Biswajit Roy and Pradeep Vyas (2005), ***"The Sunderbans"***, New Delhi: Rupa Pubication India Pvt. Ltd.

291. Sohela, Mustari (2013), "The Challenges and Coping Strategies of 'Mowal' the Honey collectors of Sunderban, Bangladesh", ***International Research Journal of Social Sciences***, vol.2 (6) 7-11.

the target of honey and wax collection to 500 quintal and 140 quintal respectively. As against this, 478 quintal and 120 quintal of honey and wax were collected earning a sum of Taka 479620.[292]

Bawalis also collect wood and golpata. The demand of golpata has always been high as it is a common material utilized for building shades and walls in rural areas adjacent to the Sundarbans. The collection of the large shiny leaves (Golpata) goes on in full swing in the Sundarbans from December 15th and continues till February 15th. This has also been an important source of revenue generation for the government of Bangladesh. For this purpose, thousands of Bawalis are employed to collect the golpata. Though, the collection limit is set at 500 maunds per boat, there has been illegal over collection. It was reported that government earned revenue of over Taka 4.7 million from 170,866 quintal of golpata during earlier time.[293]

The social structure of the entire Sundarbans is determined by their livelihoods patterns and source of income. In this poverty-stricken land, money lenders *'mohajon'* do play a very vital role.

Figure: 3.5. Mawalis on their way to Honey Collection
Source-URL: http://www.fahadkaizer.com/photos.php?albums=1

292. "Mowals Busy for Collecting Honey in Sunderbans", [online:web] Accessed 24th January 2015 URL: https://www.highbeam.com/Registration/Registration1.

293. "Golpata collection goes on in Sunderbans" (2012) [online:web] Accessed 24th January 2015 URL: http://www.thefinancialexpressbd.com/old/index.php?ref=MjBfMTJfMThfMTJfMV85MV8xNTM0NjE=.

Figure: 3.6. Mowals taking measures to Repel Honeybees

Source-URL: http://www.fahadkaizer.com/photos.php?albums=1

Figure: 3.7. Mawal attempting for Honey Collection

Source-URL: http://www.fahadkaizer.com/photos.php?albums=1

3.2.4. Management of the Sundarbans

The administrative reforms and management in the Sundarbans have been a constant process since the colonial regime. In this regard, a range of institutions and agencies were set up to conduct the affairs of Sundarbans tract.

The colonial administration notified this forest as the "Protected Forest" in December 1878. This was primarily to prevent reclamation or conversion to agriculture. By notifying these forests as 'Protected' rather than 'Reserved', the colonial administration put an option before itself. The option was that they could either lease these lands for cultivation, or they could transfer these lands for the production of timber and the management of the forest as reserved forest. Furthermore, all-residual 'Protected' forest was reclassified as the 'Reserved' forest to preclude any further encroachment on the land.[294]

Nowadays, this forested part of the Indian Sundarbans is supervised by the Director of the Sundarbans Biosphere Reserve with help of the Divisional Forest Officer of 24-Parganas (South) Forest Divisions and the Field Director of the **Sundarbans Tiger Reserve,** which came into existence in December 1973 covering an area of 2585 sq.km. (Chowdhury and Vyas 2005). India adopting the 'National Man and Biosphere Programme' (as part of the 'Man and Biosphere Programme' accepted at the General Conference of the UNESCO in 1970) declared the entire Sundarbans as the **'Sundarbans Biosphere Reserve'** in March 1989 to establish a formal mechanism to coordinate and integrate the diverse activities of conservation, research and training for creating harmony between man and environment. The human inhabited portion of the Indian Sundarbans *de jure* is not under the ambit of the Director of the Biosphere Reserve.[295]

An area of 1330.12 sq. km within the Sundarbans Tiger Reserve is designated as 'Core Area,' which in the year 1984 was declared the **'Sundarbans National Park'** where tourism and other human activities are not permissible except for scientific and management related work. The rest of the area is the 'Buffer Area,' part of which is notified as the 'Saznekhali Wildlife Sanctuary' in the year 1976. In addition to this, the Sundarbans National Park was declared a **World Heritage Site** by the United Nations Educational, Scientific and Cultural Organization (UNESCO) in 1987.[296]

---

294. Danda, Anamitra Anurag and Gayathri Srikanthan (2011), "Indian Sundarbans Delta: A Vision", ***WWF Policy Document India,*** pp.15-25.

295. Ibid.

296. The World Bank (2014), ***Building Resilience for Sustainable Development of the Sundarbans: Strategy Report,*** JS Print O Pack: New Delhi.

Indian part of Sundarbans is composed of 19 Community Development (CD) Blocks, and these two blocks come under the two separate districts of North 24-Parganas and South 24-Parganas. The Zila Parishad is the highest unit of local self-government at the district level followed by the Panchayat Samiti at the block level. And the Gram Panchayat functions at the village cluster level. Corresponding to this is civil administration, which is headed by the civil servants; civil administration of the state ends at the block level. The two departments that exert the broadest administrative influence over the delta of Indian Sundarbans are the Sundarbans Affairs Department (SAD) and the Forest Department. Furthermore, in order to address the socio-economic backwardness of this region, the Sundarbans Development Board was established in 1973. This department was replaced by the Sundarbans Affairs Department in 1994.[297]

The Bangladeshi Sundarbans consists of three wildlife Sanctuaries: Sundarbans West Wildlife Sanctuary; Sundarbans East Wildlife Sanctuary; and Sundarbans South Wildlife Sanctuary. These sanctuaries were set up in 1977 under the Bangladesh Wildlife (Preservation) (Amendment) Act, 1974.[298] Given its ecological and socio-economic significance, the Reserve Forest of the Sundarbans was named the **'Ramsar site'** in 1992.[299]These three-wildlife sanctuaries have been declared as **World Heritage Site in 1997** by the UNESCO owing to its rich ecological resources.[300] The Department of Environment

297. Danda, Anamitra Anurag and Gayathri Srikanthan (2011), "Indian Sundarbans Delta: A Vision", ***WWF Policy Document India,*** pp.15-25.

298. Amin, Muhammad Nurul and Niaz Ahmed Khan (2001), "A Primer on the Nature and Management of the Sunderbans", ***Grassroots Voice: A Journal OF Indigenous Knowledge and Development***, Vol.VI, issue: 1, pp.85-101.

299. Uddin, Md. Shams, et al. (2013), "Climate Change on the Sunderbans Mangrove ecosystem services and dependent livelihoods in Bangladesh", ***Asian Journal of Conservation Biology,*** Vol.2, N. 2: 152-156.

300. Amin, Muhammad Nurul and Niaz Ahmed Khan (2001), "A Primer on the Nature and Management of the Sunderbans", ***Grassroots Voice: A Journal OF Indigenous***

has declared 10 km buffer zone around the Reserved Forest of the Sundarbans as 'Ecologically Critical Area (ECA)' in 2010. Any kinds of developmental activities are precluded.[301]

The Bangladeshi portion of Sundarbans Forest has been classified under two Forest Divisions under the Khulna circle for managing, conserving and proper use of the natural resources of the forest. In addition to this, forest management is classified into four administrative ranges that include Satkhira, Khulna, Sarankhola and Chandpai and has 16 forest stations. This region is further divided into 55 compartments and 9 blocks.[302]

The Government of India redrafted the National Forest Policy in 1988 in order to improve the issues of the environmental sustainability, conservation, and social and economic values of forests. This policy subsequently led to the establishment of the Joint Forest Management Resolution of the 1990. Following this policy shift, the Government of West Bengal issued two specific guidelines in 1991 and 1996 for the management of the Sundarbans. These are: Mangrove Forest areas of the Sundarbans; and National Parks and Sanctuaries of the State respectively. The Government of West Bengal based on these notifications set up the community based committees to enhance the people's involvement in forest management. Therefore, two

Knowledge and Development, Vol.VI, issue: 1, pp.85-101. Bhattacharjee, Tapaleena T. et al. (2011), "The Sinking "Beauty"- Sunderbans", ***Geospatial World Forum***.Uddin, Md. Shams, et al. (2013), "Climate Change on the Sunderbans Mangrove ecosystem services and dependent livelihoods in Bangladesh", ***Asian Journal of Conservation Biology***, Vol.2, N. 2: 152-156.

301. Uddin, Md. Shams, et al. (2013), "Climate Change on the Sunderbans Mangrove ecosystem services and dependent livelihoods in Bangladesh", ***Asian Journal of Conservation Biology***, Vol.2, N. 2: 154.

302. "The Great Sunderbans (Bangladesh and India): Forest swamp, draw only border, UNESCO World Heritage Site', [Online: web] Accessed 24th January 2015 URL: http://wikimapia.org/1651148/The-Great-Sundarbans-Bangladesh-and-India.

committees, viz. 51 Forest Protection Committees; and 14 Eco Development Committees were set up.[303]

For the usage and management of the Sundarbans, many projects were launched that included: Nipa Project, Cotton Project, Sunflower Project, Tourism Development Project, Coconut Development Project, Fisheries Project, Tiger Reserve Project, Crocodile Rearing and Breeding Project and Sundarbans Delta Project. Some organizations working for the management of the Sundarbans are either financed by the Government or by some voluntary agencies. These include River Research Institute, Govt. of WB; United Nations Development Programme (UNDP) at Sushama Devi Chaudhurani Marine Biology Research Station; Marine Product Export Development Authority (MPEDA); Socio-economic Development Programme (SEDP); Lok Siksha Parishad, Ramkrishna Mission, Narendrapur; Ramkrishna Mission, Nimpith and the Krishi Vigyan Kendra and West Bengal Agricultural Extension Wings; Some ICAR organizations like Central Soil Salinity Research Station, Canning; Central Inland Fisheries Research Station, Kakdwip; All India Coordinated Project on Brackishwater Pisciculture, Barrackpur; Jute Agricultural Research Station, Gosaba and Krishi Vigyan Kendra, Kakdwip.[304]

In addition to this, Sagar Gramin Bank, headquarter at Amtala, and various branches of the State Bank, and United Bank of India have been engaged in the empowerment of the inhabitants of the Sundarbans.[305]

---

303. Danda, Anamitra Anurag and Gayathri Srikanthan (2011), "Indian Sundarbans Delta: A Vision", ***WWF Policy Document India,*** p.15.

304. Naskar, Kumudranjan and D. N. Guha Bakshi (1987), ***Mangrove Swamps of the Sundarbans: an Ecological Perspective,*** Calcutta: Naya Prokash, 207-09.

305. Ibid.

Chapter Four

Impact of Climate Change on Sundarbans

The climate of the earth is constantly changing over time as it is evident and many scientific studies have corroborated these changing phenomena. Nevertheless, what exactly caused the advent of climate change is widely debated at both the scientific and the political fora. The Intergovernmental Panel on Climate Change (IPCC) 2007 attributed this phenomenon of global warming induced climate change largely to the anthropogenic activities.[306] Every nook and corner of the globe is experiencing the irrevocable impact of climate change. Some parts of the world, especially low-lying coastal region have been the most adversely affected by this phenomenon. India and Bangladesh have been identified among the 27 countries most vulnerable to the climate change induced accelerated sea level rise. The tract of Sundarbans spanning over India and Bangladesh does not remain exception to these changes.

The decreasing freshwater flow from Himalayan rivers predicted for the dry season (dry season getting drier), gradual increase in sea level and the likely enhancement of the severity of salinity ingression in the Sundarbans could be rather very regressive. This has also enhanced the process of coastal erosion jeopardizing the existence of the Sundarbans. Though the process of erosion and accretion have

306. Danda, Anamitra Anurag and Gayathri Srikanthan (2011), "Indian Sundarbans Delta: A Vision", ***WWF Policy Document India,*** pp.1-40.

been a natural phenomenon, certain well evident pattern of changes in climate and anthropogenic activities in recent years have added to these natural phenomena aggravating situation in the whole tract of Sundarbans.

The tract of Sundarbans, depicted as a wonderful 'barometer of change'[307] is both unique and uniquely fragile.[308] It is unique owing to the existence of one of the most extensive forest of mangrove in the world lying in a vast deltaic place where freshwater and seawater mingle; and also because of the presence of an endangered species like Royal Bengal Tiger, and human habitation. Moreover, it is ironical that Sundarbans' fragility protrudes from its uniqueness aggravated by the climate change. Mahadevia and Vikash stated that the Sundarbans being an innocent victim of burgeoning global warming and climate change faces a direct threat to its very existence.[309]

4.1. The Changing Climate of the Sundarbans

It is rather difficult to attribute the present changes in the Sundarbans directly and wholly to the problem of climate change. However, the changes in the Sundarbans are highly perceptible in respect of changes in sea surface temperature, precipitation pattern, occurrence of extreme weather events, and changes in the sea level.[310]

---

307. "Sunderban is Sick: 40% Forest Affected by Top-Dying", ***Earth Touch***, No.3/ February 1997.

308. WWF Report India (2010), "Sundarbans: Future Imperfect- Climate Adaptation Report", pp.1-28.

309. Mahadevia, Kanksha and Mayank Vikash, "Climate change-Impact on the Sunderbans: A case Study", ***International Scientific Journal Environmental Science,*** [Online: web] Accessed 7 July 2015 URL: http://environment.scientific-journal.com/articles/2/1.pdf.

310. Danda, Anamitra Anurag and Gayathri Srikanthan (2011), "Indian Sundarbans Delta: A Vision", ***WWF Policy Document India,*** pp.1-40.

4.1.1. Changes in Temperature

Over the past three decades, the temperature of the water in the Bay of Bengal has been constantly increasing. The increase in the sea surface temperature (SST) has been much higher than the global average temperature, and this increase is even higher than the Arabian Sea on the western coast of India (CSE 2012).[311] In this sense, Eastern coastal region is more vulnerable than the western coastal region to the onslaught of global warming induced climate changes. The observed rise in the surface air temperature is 0.019°C per year over the Bay of Bengal during the period 1985 to 2000, and the same rising trend is seen in the Sundarbans.[312] It is further observed that if this trend continues, the temperature in this area is expected to rise by more than 1°C by 2050;[313] and it is likely to cross the threshold of 2°C rise by 2100.[314] Between 1980 and 2007, the SST in the Sundarbans has been found to be accelerating at the rate of 0.5°C per decade, eight times the rate of globally observed SST warming of 0.06°C per decade[315] that

311. Center for Science and Environment (2012), "Living with changing climate: Impact, vulnerability and adaptation challenges in Indian Sundarbans".

312. WWF Report India (2010), "Sundarbans: Future Imperfect- Climate Adaptation Report", pp.1-28. Danda, Anamitra Anurag and Gayathri Srikanthan (2011), "Indian Sundarbans Delta: A Vision", ***WWF Policy Document India***, pp.1-40; Hazra Sugata, "Climate Change Policy paper II: Climate Change Adaptation in Coastal Region of West Bengal"; Bose, Sahana, "Human Influence on Mangrove Ecosystem in Indian Sunderbans: An Earth Atmospheric Interaction".

313. WWF Report India (2010), "Sundarbans: Future Imperfect- Climate Adaptation Report", pp.1-28; Hazra Sugata, "Climate Change Policy paper II: Climate Change Adaptation in Coastal Region of West Bengal".

314. Hazra Sugata, "Climate Change Policy paper II: Climate Change Adaptation in Coastal Region of West Bengal", p.5.

315. Center for Science and Environment (2012), "Living with changing climate: Impact, vulnerability and adaptation challenges in Indian Sundarbans"; Mahadevia, Kanksha and Mayank Vikash, "Climate change-Impact on the Sunderbans: A case Study", ***International Scientific Journal Environmental Science,*** [Online: web] Accessed 7 July 2015 URL: http://environment.scientific-journal.com/articles/2/1.pdf;Gupta, Subhadip and Gargi Sarkar (2014), "Climate Change and Economic

made the Sundarbans one of the worst climate change hotspots in the world.

A joint study over changes in SST in Sundarbans was conducted by a team of researchers from Massachusetts Institute of Technology and University of Calcutta in 2009. The study found that the average temperature in the pre-monsoon period have increased from 31°C to 31.6°C between 1980 to 2007.[316] The Indian Meteorological Department (IMD) in 2009 had analyzed an increase in SST in Sundarbans for all three seasons, i.e. pre-monsoon, monsoon and winters. This study observed that the SST in all three seasons was higher in comparison to what had been a few decades earlier in the Bay of Bengal.[317] It is widely believed that the acceleration in the SST can have links with the frequency of cyclones in this region. This changing ambience is causing grave impacts on the moribund delta, and the mangrove forest encompassing the aquatic life, which is more sensitive to these changes.

4.1.2. Changes in the Intensity of Precipitation

There is a pervasive consensus on the fact that precipitation pattern will be changed in the wake of global warming. The Center for Science and Environment (CSE) stated that the exact nature of this kind of

---

Adaptability of Indian Sunderban", ***Journal of Economic and Sustainable Development***, Vol.5, No. 22; Mitra, A. et al. (2009), " Observed changes in water mass properties in the Indian Sundarbans (northwestern Bay of Bengal) during 1980–2007", ***Current Science***, Vol. 97, No. 10, pp. 1445-1452. Quoted in Haq, Syed Azizul (2010), ***"Impact of Climate Change on "Sunderbans", The Largest Mangrove Forest: Ways Forward"***, a paper presented at the 18th Commonwealth Forestry Conference 2010, 28 June-02 July 2010, Edinburgh International Conference Center, Scotland UK.

316. Center for Science and Environment (2012), "Living with changing climate: Impact, vulnerability and adaptation challenges in Indian Sundarbans"; Gupta, Subhadip and Gargi Sarkar (2014), "Climate Change and Economic Adaptability of Indian Sunderban", ***Journal of Economic and Sustainable Development***, Vol.5, No.22.

317. Center for Science and Environment (2012), "Living with changing climate: Impact, vulnerability and adaptation challenges in Indian Sundarbans".

change over Sundarbans is not yet pellucid. On the other hand, WWF India (2010) considers that there has been an agreement over changes in the precipitation patterns over the Sundarbans.

The Indian Meteorological Department (IMD) observed significant increase in the rainfall over Bay of Bengal, with the marked increase in the rainy days along with the intensity of rains and risk of flooding as well in 2007.[318] Even the analysis carried out by the WWF India (2010) from the study period 1990 to 2000 and 2001 to 2008 found increasing trend of rainfall over the Bay of Bengal and Sundarbans.[319]

The marginal increase in the monsoon and post-monsoon rainfall has been observed during the study period of 1990 to 2000; and the annual average rainfall over Sundarbans is recorded at 1625 mm, which during the high rainfall years goes up to 2000 mm and falls to 1300 mm in low rainfall years.[320] In 2009, a study undertaken by the School of Oceanographic Studies, Jadavpur University observed that the intensity of rainfall over the Bay of Bengal has accelerated at the rate of 0.0041 mm/hr and that resulted in the marginal increase in the average annual rainfall in the region of Bay of Bengal.[321] This is also in conformity with the above mentioned finding by the WWF.

The scientists from the IMD in 2009 analyzing the impact of SST increase on rainfall observed that "the total frequency of low-pressure systems that cause rainfall has neither increased nor decreased significantly; rather the duration of these rain-bearing systems have increased significantly bereft of actually resulting into rainfall. The

318. Ibid.

319. WWF Report India (2010), "Sundarbans: Future Imperfect- Climate Adaptation Report", pp.1-28.

320. Ibid.

321. Center for Science and Environment (2012), "Living with changing climate: Impact, vulnerability and adaptation challenges in Indian Sundarbans".

acceleration in the SST leads to the greater evaporation and excess increase in this process beyond the certain threshold is not propitious for the precipitation, and affects the rainfall negatively. The increase in SST is observed to be leading longer but drier monsoon that causes a single rainfall events becoming more intense."[322] It is expected that during the dry season the impacts of climate change on the Sundarbans would be more perilous extending from November to April as the climate models' prediction observes decrease in the precipitation.[323] Bose has stated, "Rainfall has significantly increased and became more erratic within a span of ten years over the Sundarbans and the period of monsoon has shifted; in the sense, it is delayed by 15 to 20 days."[324]

4.1.3. Changes in the Frequency and Magnitude of the Extreme Weather Events

WWF Policy Document (2011) observes, "Cyclones are rare in Bay of Bengal from January to March. In April and May, these form in the south and adjoining central Bay and move initially northwest, north and then recurve to the northeast often striking the Arakan coast in April and Andhra-Orissa-West Bengal-Bangladesh coasts in May. Most of the monsoon (June -September) storms develop in the central and in the north Bay and move west-northwestwards affecting Andhra-Orissa-West Bengal coasts. Post monsoon (October-December) storms form mostly in the south and the central Bay, recurve between 15°and 18° N affecting Tamil Nadu-Andhra Orissa-West Bengal-Bangladesh coasts."[325]

---

322. Ibid.

323. Minar, M. H. et al. (2013), "Climate Change and Coastal Zone of Bangladesh: Vulnerability, Resilience and Adaptability", ***Middle-East Journal of Scientific Research***, 13 (1): 114-120.

324. Bose, Sahana, "Human Influence on Mangrove Ecosystem in Indian Sunderbans: An Earth Atmospheric Interaction".

325. Danda, Anamitra Anurag and Gayathri Srikanthan (2011), "Indian Sundarbans Delta: A Vision", ***WWF Policy Document India***, pp.1-40.

The changes in the frequency of cyclonic activities and its magnitude have turned out to be more calamitous in the climatic patterns of the Sundarbans. A consensus is found among the various researchers on the issue of magnitude of cyclonic activities. They consider that there transpired changes in the local weather;[326] and the frequency of severe cyclonic storm has actually decreased, however severity of these cyclones have gone up, possibly as a corollary of rising SST.[327] Mahadevia and Vikash have noted that between 1951 and 2010 the increase in the intensity of cyclonic storms has been observed hitting the Sundarbans.[328] Furthermore, a study by WWF India (2010) also reported the same trends of declining storms' frequency and cyclone in the Bay of Bengal over the period from 1970 to 2000, with an increase in its magnitude.[329]

A pattern in the robustness of the storms has also been felt that vary from season to season. For instance, pre- and post-monsoon storms were found to be stronger than the storms that were observed in the monsoon season. Life span of a severe cyclonic storm in the Indian Sea averages about 4 days from the time it takes cyclonic shape until the time it approaches the land. Over the last 120 years, 26% increases in severe cyclonic storms over the Bay of Bengal have been registered that is found to be intensifying in the post-monsoon period.[330]

326. Bose, Sahana, "Human Influence on Mangrove Ecosystem in Indian Sunderbans: An Earth Atmospheric Interaction".

327. Hazra et al. (2002), "Sea Level and associated changes in the Sunderbans", ***Science and Culture,*** vol.68, no 9-12, pp.309-321.

328. Mahadevia, Kanksha and Mayank Vikash, "Climate change-Impact on the Sunderbans: A case Study", ***International Scientific Journal Environmental Science,*** [Online: web] Accessed 7 July 2015 URL: http://environment.scientific-journal.com/articles/2/1.pdf.

329. WWF Report India (2010), "Sundarbans: Future Imperfect- Climate Adaptation Report", pp.1-28.

330. Singh, O. P. (2007), 'Spatial variation of sea level trend along the Bangladesh coast', ***Mar Geol,*** Vol 25, pp. 205-212; Singh, O.P. (2007), "Long-term trends in the Frequency of severe cyclones of Bay of Bengal: Observations and simulations",

Figure: 4.1. Cyclone Sidr

Densely populated low-lying coastal areas of the Sundarbans are highly susceptible to extreme weather events such as cyclone Sidr (WWF India 2010).

As per the records of 1964 storms' decadal frequency in the Bay of Bengal from the period 1891 to 1961 as carried out by the IMD shows 56 cyclones occurred during 1921-1930, while 32 storms were observed for the period 1951-1960s.[331] In the Sundarbans as the studies have shown that over the past 120 years the frequency of cyclones from high to very high intensity cyclones has increased by 26%.[332] The

---

Mausam, 58(16), pp.59-66; Center for Science and Environment (2012), "Living with changing climate: Impact, vulnerability and adaptation challenges in Indian Sundarbans"; WWF Report India (2010), "Sunderbans: Future Imperfect- Climate Adaptation Report"; Danda, Anamitra Anurag and Gayathri Srikanthan (2011), "Indian Sundarbans Delta: A Vision", ***WWF Policy Document India.***pp.1-40.

331. Gopinath, G. and P Seralathan 2005, "Rapid coastal erosion of the Sagar Island, West Bengal", ***Environmental***

Geology, Springer Berlin Heidelberg. Vol. 48 No. 8, p. 1058-1067; Center for Science and Environment (2012), "Living with changing climate: Impact, vulnerability and adaptation challenges in Indian Sundarbans"; Danda, Anamitra Anurag and Gayathri Srikanthan (2011), "Indian Sundarbans Delta: A Vision", ***WWF Policy Document India.*** pp.1-40.

332. Singh, O. P. (2007), 'Long-term trends in the frequency of severe cyclones of Bay of Bengal: Observations and simulations', ***Mausam***, Vol 58, No 1, pp. 59-66; Center for Science and Environment (2012), "Living with changing climate: Impact,

Sundarbans has experienced 4 cyclones from 2007 to 2009, viz. Sidr, Nargis, Bijli, and Aila.[333] Aila even destroyed the oldest recorded spring water based river systems in Bhutan.[334]

4.1.4. Rising Trends of Sea Level

The rise in the level of sea is another prominent threat for the existence of the Sundarbans. The rising trends of the sea level have jeopardized the future viability of the Sundarbans. That there is lack of unanimity among researcher on the real extent and magnitude of this change in the sea level is clearly apparent. However, an agreement among the researcher on the issue of sea level rise adjoining to the Sundarbans areas can be observed. Like the increase in the sea surface temperature, the rate of relative sea level rise in Sundarbans has also been observed to be higher than the global average rate of sea level rise. This has occurred due to a combination of factors on which the entire dynamics of any delta and coastline depends, namely compaction and tectonic subsidence, relative sea level rise and wave action, and finally supply of sediment from the rivers.[335] The deltaic region of Sundarbans exhibits all the above features. However, the exact reason is not observed in case of sea level rise in an Indian Sundarbans;[336] for the Bangladeshi

---

vulnerability and adaptation challenges in Indian Sundarbans"; Danda, Anamitra Anurag and Gayathri Srikanthan (2011), "Indian Sundarbans Delta: A Vision", ***WWF Policy Document Indi,*** pp.1-40.

333. Danda, Anamitra Anurag and Gayathri Srikanthan (2011), "Indian Sundarbans Delta: A Vision", ***WWF Policy Document Indi,*** pp.1-40.

334. Lama, Mahendra P (2015), email to the author, 25 July 2015.

335. Raha, Atanu et al. (2012), "Climate Change impacts on Indian Sunderbans: a time series analysis (1924-2008)", ***Biodivers Conserve,*** 21: 1289-1307.

336. Mitra,A. et al. (2009), "Pulse of climate change in Sunderbans: a myth or reality?" ***Natl Acad Sci Lett*** 32:1-2. Quoted in Raha, Atanu et al. (2012), "Climate Change impacts on Indian Sunderbans: a time series analysis (1924-2008)", ***Biodivers Conserve,*** 21: 1289-1307.

Sundarbans, the monsoonal rains and land subsidence are found as a major dominant factor.[337]

A recent report of the School of Oceanographic Studies, Jadavpur University, Kolkata observed the increase of sea level rise at 17.8 mm/year between 2000 and 2009.[338] Furthermore, the research conducted by the National Institute of Oceanography, Goa, in 2006 found an increase of 5.7 mm/year in sea level between the year 2000 and 2004.[339] A tide assessment data from the period 1985 to 1998 at Sagar island observatory revealed rises in relative mean sea level at 3.14 mm/year[340] that is greater than the similar trend of average global sea level rise of 2 mm/year. The same rising trend of 3.14 mm/year was also observed from the period 1985 to 2000[341] and global estimation of sea level rise was found between 0.5 to 3 mm/year.[342] Furthermore, it was predicted that by 2050, the present trend of relative sea level rise of 3.14 mm/year would lead to 1-meter rise.[343]

---

337. Singh, O.P. (2002), "Spatial variation of sea level trend along the Bangladesh coast", ***Mar Geol***, 25: 205-212. Quoted in Raha, Atanu et al. (2012), "Climate Change impacts on Indian Sunderbans: a time series analysis (1924-2008)", ***Biodivers Conserve***, 21: 1289-1307.

338. Hazra, S. et al. (2010), 'Temporal Change Detection (2001-2008) Study of Sundarban', School of Oceanographic Studies, Jadavpur University, Kolkata.

339. Unnikrishnan, A.S. et al (2006), 'Sea level changes along the Indian coast: observations and projections', ***Current Science***, Vol. 90 No. 3, pp. 362-368.

340. Hazra et al. (2002), "Sea Level and associated changes in the Sunderbans", ***Science and Culture,*** vol.68, no 9-12, pp.309-321.

341. WWF Report India (2010), "Sundarbans: Future Imperfect- Climate Adaptation Report", pp.1-28.

342. Warrick, R.A. and Oerlemans, J. (1990).Sea level rise. In 'Climate Change: The IPCC Scientific Assessment', Houghton, J.T., Jenkins, G.J. and Ephraums, J.J. (Ed.), Cambridge University Press, p. 257-281; Hazra et al. (2002), "Sea Level and associated changes in the Sunderbans", ***Science and Culture,*** vol.68, no 9-12, pp.309-321; WWF Report India (2010), "Sundarbans: Future Imperfect- Climate Adaptation Report".

343. Hazra et al. (2002), "Sea Level and associated changes in the Sunderbans", ***Science and Culture,*** vol.68, no 9-12, pp.309-321.

The SAARC Meteorological Research Centre (SMRC) in Dhaka using the tidal gauge records from 1977 to 1998 observed that sea level was rising with increasing east-west trend of 4 mm- 7.8 mm per year.[344] In the Hooghly river estuary, the analysis of 50 years of data at the Permanent Service for Mean Sea Level (PSMSL) reveals sea level rises of between +0.76 mm/year and +5.22 mm/year at various locations in the Sundarbans.[345]

4.2. Impact of Climate Change on Various Social Aspects of the Sundarbans

The above discussed climate change induced drivers of change have its profound impact on various aspects of the Sundarbans. These include changes in the mangrove forest cover, biodiversity, wildlife diversity and behavior, changes in the human settlement, embankment failure, effects on resource dependent livelihood. Sea level rise, increasing salinity pattern, constant coastal erosion, flooding and submergence of the island along with the intense extreme weather events have caused massive upheaval in the geography of Sundarbans. The man-made related anthropogenic factors like increasing population, widespread exploitation of natural resources, deforestation, and reclamation have also been responsible to the large extent as it is evident through the various studies on the Sundarbans. The evidences of the onslaught of the climate change induced drivers of change have been found to be adding fuel to the fire.

---

344. Alam, M. (2003), "Bangladesh Country case study", National Adaptation Programme of Action (NAPA) Workshop, Bhutan, pp.9-11; Loucks, Colby et al. (2010), "Sea level rise and tigers: predicted impacts to Bangladesh's Sunderbans mangroves", ***Climatic Change***, 98: 291-298.

345. Nandy, S. and S. Bandyopadhyay (2008), "Trend of sea level change in the Hugli Estuary, West Bengal", ***Souvenir and Abstracts Volume***, 21st Conference of Indian Institute of Geomorphology, Tripura University, pp. 83-84; Danda, Anamitra Anurag and Gayathri Srikanthan (2011), "Indian Sundarbans Delta: A Vision", ***WWF Policy Document Indi,*** p.1-40; Center for Science and Environment (2012), "Living with changing climate: Impact, vulnerability and adaptation challenges in Indian Sundarbans".

4.2.1. Mangrove Forest

Mangrove forests of the Sundarbans, apart from the anthropogenic factors, is even largely affected by the climate-induced changes in temperature, precipitation, frequent inundation, intense cyclone, sea level rise and increasing salinity throughout the tract. The IPCC has projected that the state of tropical forest ecosystems is all set to get worst in the wake of climate change. Bangladesh being in the tropical region will face these phenomena.[346] Various studies have shown that tropical cyclones, to the great extent, devour the mangrove forest of the Sundarbans, i.e., in the recent past, a cyclone like Sidr destroyed one-third of the Sundarbans.[347]

The WWF conducted a study from the period 1990 to 2000 and 2000 to 2009 ascertaining the ground reality of the forest cover change in the Indian Sundarbans. The 1990 to 2000 study stated that the total area of the Sundarbans combined with Indian and Bangladeshi part until the year 1770 was 36,000 sq. km. It was measured to be 25,000 sq. km in the year 2000. The Indian part of Sundarbans occupied 9,630 sq. km out of which 4,264 sq. km constituted reserve forests. In addition, out of this portion mangrove forest held 2,168 sq. km and tidal rivers held 2,096 sq. km. The study from 2000 to 2009 observed that the forest cover in the Indian Sundarbans has declined to 2,132 sq. km from 2,168 sq. km. Furthermore, this study delineated that the level of saline blanks have grown significantly from 38.93 sq. km to 74.79 sq. km that affects the physicality of the forest.[348]

---

346. Haq, Syed Azizul (2010), ***"Impact of Climate Change on "Sunderbans", The Largest Mangrove Forest: Ways Forward"***, a paper presented at the 18th Commonwealth Forestry Conference 2010, 28 June-02 July 2010, Edinburgh International Conference Center, Scotland UK. p.8.

347. Ibid.8

348. WWF Report India (2010), "Sundarbans: Future Imperfect- Climate Adaptation Report", pp.1-28.

The pattern of salinity inside the forest will change considerably because of climate change.[349] There is a growing consensus among the scholars that intrusion of saline water due to reduction of freshwater flow upstream backed up by the sea level rise has been the major factor for the loss of this euphonious vegetative tract of mangrove forest.

To comprehend the magnitude and pattern of the declining forest, the Sundarbans can be divided into three distinct ecological zone based on the degree of salinity where tree species vary in accordance with the changes in salinity.[350] These are as follows: *Oligohaline Zone* (relatively freshwater or less saline water) with salinity level 5-15 ppt (parts per thousand); *Mesohaline Zone* (moderately saline) with salinity level 15-25 ppt; and *Polyhaline Zone* (saline or strong saline zone) with salinity level 25-30 ppt. The dominant species grown in the *oligohaline zone* is Sundari (*Heriteira fomes*) which is the most valuable timber in the forest account for over 60% of the unalloyed volume of commercial timber. In the *mesohaline zone*, the dominant species is Gewa (*Excoecaria agallocha*), and the low height Goran (*Ceriops decandra*) grows up in the *polyhaline zone.*[351]

---

349. Minar, M. H. et al. (2013), "Climate Change and Coastal Zone of Bangladesh: Vulnerability, Resilience and Adaptability", ***Middle-East Journal of Scientific Research,*** 13 (1): 114-120.

350. Salinity threatens the world Heritage "The Sunderban of Bangladesh"- Published by PRDI-***Participatory Research and Development Initiative.*** URL:**http://www.preventionweb.net/files/8203_SalinityandMangrove.pdf**; Hussain, Mohammad Asad et al. (2013), "Changes of the Seasonal Salinity Distribution at the Sundarbans Coast due to Impact of climate change", 4th International Conference on Water & Flood Management (ICWFM-2013), pp.637-648.

351. Salinity threatens the world Heritage "The Sunderban of Bangladesh"- Published by PRDI-***Participatory Research and Development Initiative.*** URL:**http://www.preventionweb.net/files/8203_SalinityandMangrove.pdf**; Hussain, Mohammad Asad et al. (2013), "Changes of the Seasonal Salinity Distribution at the Sundarbans Coast due to Impact of climate change", 4th International Conference on Water & Flood Management (ICWFM-2013), pp.637-648.

Scientists suspect that due to the onslaught of the global warming the world's greatest mangrove forest is sick[352] owing to the possible sea level rise induced salinity. It is assessed by the WWF that owing to the sea level rise, near about 7,500 hectares of mangrove forest in the Bangladeshi Sundarbans is projected to be flooded.[353] The impact of Salinity is a significant factor in determining the distribution of species and productivity of the mangrove forest of the Sundarbans considerably.[354] Terry Thomas who considered that tidal rise changes vegetative composition and its distribution also vindicates this; and tree growth is noticed to be regulated by the tidal level.[355] It is observed that with the increasing pattern of salinity level in the Bangladeshi Sundarbans from east to west, the density of vegetation growth, its height and canopy decreases from east to west.[356] Moreover, with an increase in salinity level, a significant decrease in regeneration and growth is also observed which indicates that germination is linked to salinity.[357]

---

352. The term "sick" indicates the abysmal condition of the Sundarbans forest that due to possibly climate change impact is in wane. "Sunderban is Sick: 40% Forest Affected by Top-Dying", ***Earth Touch***, No.3/February 1997, p.9.

353. Haq, Syed Azizul (2010), ***"Impact of Climate Change on "Sunderbans", The Largest Mangrove Forest: Ways Forward"***, a paper presented at the 18th Commonwealth Forestry Conference 2010, 28 June-02 July 2010, Edinburgh International Conference Center, Scotland UK

354. Das, S. and Siddiqi, N.A. (1985), "The mangroves and mangrove forest of Bangladesh", Mangrove Silviculture Divison, Bulletin No.2, Bangladesh Forest Research Institute, Mangrove plantations of the coastal afforestation project. UNDP Project BGD/85/085, Dhaka, Field document No.2, p.69. Raha, Atanu et al. (2012), "Climate Change impacts on Indian Sunderbans: a time series analysis (1924-2008)", ***Biodivers Conserve***, 21: 1289-1307.

355. "Sunderban is Sick: 40% Forest Affected by Top-Dying", ***Earth Touch***, No.3/ February 1997, p.9.

356. Hussain, Mohammad Asad et al. (2013), "Changes of the Seasonal Salinity Distribution at the Sundarbans Coast due to Impact of climate change", 4th International Conference on Water & Flood Management (ICWFM-2013), pp.637-648.

357. Siddique, N.A. (2001), "Mangrove Forestry in Bangladesh", Institute of Forestry & Environmental Sciences, University of Chittagong. Quoted in Hussain, Mohammad

It is estimated that as a corollary of salinity ingression in the Sundarbans, the most of the moderately saline area will transform into strong saline area and the possibility is that less freshwater areas would decline to the large extent along the lower Baleshwar River in the eastern part of the forest. Due to the constant intrusion of salinity deeper into the Sundarbans, there is possibility that one type of area with different level of salinity pattern and plant species would be replaced by another level of salinity and species. For instance, the Sundari tree grows up in the freshwater area could be replaced by Gewa; and Gewa could be replaced by less valuable Goran. With the combined disappearance of both freshwater and moderately saline water area, the Sundarbans would lose its over 50% of merchantable wood. The existing poor productivity of the Indian side of Sundarbans' forest would further suffer a setback with the increasing trend of salinity.[358] The reduction in the merchantable wood would directly affect the various needs of the masses. Most importantly, the reduction in this kind of wood would hamper the commercial market. The demands of the commodities made from this wood would go up because of the shortages, which in many ways would affect the needs of the people. In other way, merchantable wood loss will lead to impact on economic activities, livelihood pattern and other forward and backward linkages. It could lead to under-utilization of factory capacities and displacement of people with serious social and political implications.

The climate change will have its impact also upon the supporting service of the Sundarbans. A study reveals that with 32 cm SLR by

---

Asad et al. (2013), "Changes of the Seasonal Salinity Distribution at the Sundarbans Coast due to Impact of climate change", 4th International Conference on Water & Flood Management (ICWFM-2013), pp.637-648.

358. Salinity threatens the world Heritage "The Sunderban of Bangladesh"- Published by PRDI-*Participatory Research and Development Initiative.* URL:**http://www.preventionweb.net/files/8203_SalinityandMangrove.pdf;** Minar, M.H. et al. (2013), "Climate Change and Coastal Zone of Bangladesh: Vulnerability, Resilience and Adaptability", ***Middle-East Journal of Scientific Research***, 13 (1): 114-120.

2050, the area of Sundari tree would reduce by 14% and 45% by 2100; on the other hand, by 2100 the appropriate area of 'Gewa' would shrink maximum 7% owing to rises in sea level. Moreover, due to the climate change impact the forest dependent diverse wildlife habitat would be highly exposed.

Another area of concern has been in the top dying[359] of the mangrove forest that has emerged at the forefront, which is linked with the increasing level of salinity. Scientists argue that about 40 % of the 5,800 sq. km. of the forest fringing the Bay of Bengal is affected by the 'Top dying' which kills off the mangrove forest from the top down.[360] Terry Thomas expressed concerns over the magnitude of the top dying and mentioned that if this is the true case in regard to the mangrove forest of the Sundarbans then nothing can be done to protect the forest that will further leave the Bangladesh to face the decimated fishing industry, increased flooding and the loss of endangered animals.[361]

The sick mangrove forest further made him realize that global warming might be having an impact on the rising trend of sea level in the Bay of Bengal.[362] Haq argued that the adverse effects of the burgeoning salinity on the ecosystem of the Sundarbans are manifested

---

359. Top dying is a sort of disease that strikes the forest trees selectively with deadly effects starting from the top of the tree. The inception of this disease begins with the dark green branches hanging limply. Between five weeks to three years, the branches are betided yellow and then further turn brown. The weakened tree soon sheds its needless and stops growing new branches. It happens to be leafless at the top and appears stunted. And finally drought, insects and parasite mangle the weakened plant; Definition of the top dying is taken from the: (Khan, M.A. 2006. Depletion of forest cover portends climatic disaster. ***The Daily Star***, Dhaka. Quoted. in Haq, Syed Azizul (2010), ***"Impact of Climate Change on "Sunderbans", The Largest Mangrove Forest: Ways Forward"***, a paper presented at the 18th Commonwealth Forestry Conference 2010, 28 June-02 July 2010, Edinburgh International Conference Center, Scotland UK.

360. "Sunderban is Sick: 40% Forest Affected by Top-Dying", ***Earth Touch***, No.3/ February 1997, p.9.

361. Ibid.9.

362. Ibid.9.

in the dying of tops of Sundari trees, retrogression of forest types, slow forest growth, and declined productivity of the forest sites.[363]

However, for the cause of top dying diseases increasing salinity cannot be solely responsible. This may be a synergic effect of assorted factors encompassing salinity, sedimentation, water logging, cyclone damage, and accumulation of toxic elements from agricultural waste and port discharge.[364] Salinity ingression into Sundarbans can be said to have inflicted major dominant impacts on the forest among all other factors, and this is what exactly seems evident from the above made arguments discussed by various researchers.

4.2.2. Mangrove Bio-diversity

Climate change has become a major threat to the ecosystem and the bio-diversity of the Sundarbans. The increasing trend of the sea level and decreasing freshwater flow particularly during the winter when Sundarbans goes through scanty rainfall will cause inland intrusion of saline water. Many mangrove species being intolerant of soaring salinity, because of these changes, may be threatened. Moreover, the dense human population just outside the fringes of the forest would further stymie the migration of this mangrove area to less saline areas making the situation more complex. The Sundarbans may be swamped entirely with a one-meter increase in sea level. The increase in temperature and sea level will gravely affect the mangrove biodiversity.[365]

---

363. Haq, Syed Azizul (2010), *"Impact of Climate Change on "Sunderbans", The Largest Mangrove Forest: Ways Forward"*, a paper presented at the 18th Commonwealth Forestry Conference 2010, 28 June-02 July 2010, Edinburgh International Conference Center, Scotland UK.

364. Ibid.7.

365. Salinity threatens the world Heritage "The Sunderban of Bangladesh"- Published by PRDI-*Participatory Research and Development Initiative.* URL:**http://www.preventionweb.net/files/8203_SalinityandMangrove.pdf.**

Figure: 4.2. Loss of Biodiversity due to cyclone Aila in 2009
Source-URL:http://images.indianexpress.com/2009/06/m_id_84457_aila.jpg?w=300.

With the shrinking of the mangrove area, many floral and faunal species may face extinction because they may not be equipped to adapt to such new environmental changes. Freshwater stress during winter and the excess water during summer will have its significant effects on the ecosystem and biodiversity of the Sundarbans. A wide range of species of mammals, birds, amphibians, reptiles, crustaceans, and above all the Royal Bengal Tiger will face the brunt of being extinct. About the floral species, the perils posed by the onset of the climate changes is apparent where top dying of the floral species especially the Sundari tree have become a matter of concern. The soil salinity will increase due to a combination of high evapo-transpiration and low flow of freshwater in winter. As a result, the freshwater loving species will be severely affected. The degradation of the forest quality may lead to the depletion of rich diversity of the Sundarbans' flora and fauna.[366] Loucks et al. (2010) have hinted that climate change induced fear of habitation loss owing to the rises in sea level may result in the tigers joining the polar bear as an early victim.[367]

---

366. Ibid.

367. Loucks, Colby et al. (2010), "Sea level rise and tigers: predicted impacts to Bangladesh's Sunderbans mangroves", ***Climatic Change***, 98: 291-298.

4.2.2.1. Man-animal conflict

The conflict between man and animal is not a recent process in the vast swathes of the Sundarbans. However, fast changing ground reality inside the forest and its vicinities in the wake of climate change has enhanced this process of man-animal conflict. With the adverse impacts of climate change on the production of biomass and fruits on which the wild animals thrive and sustain, and with the loss of land to the sea, the situation has culminated into an increased threat to animals coming into a greater conflict with man outside the forest.[368] The extremely high human density on the forest fringes causes extremely high biotic pressure such as fishing, illicit felling and prawn seed collection. Along the western boundary of the Sundarbans Tiger Reserve and north-western fringes of 24 Parganas (South) forest division, the Tigers often stray into the villages resulting in acute man-animal conflict.[369] A conflict situation has always been detrimental for both man and animal and has culminated into death of either side. This situation has become a threat to the existence of critically endangered Royal Bengal Tigers. Owing to the fear of man eating, tigers are often killed by the villagers.[370] For Instance, a report of Sundarbans forest division pointed that the people killed at least 145 tigers from 1972 to 2008. The highest killings of the tigers have been reported in the Chandpai Range of the Sundarbans division. The official also gets report of tiger killing on an average basis from Khulna and Satkhira region.[371]

---

368. Mahadevia, Kanksha and Mayank Vikash, "Climate change-Impact on the Sunderbans: A case Study", ***International Scientific Journal Environmental Science,*** [Online: web] Accessed 7 July 2015 URL: http://environment.scientific-journal.com/articles/2/1.pdf.

369. Chowdhury, Biswajit Roy, and Pradeep Vyas (2005), "The Sunderbans: A Pictorial Field Guide",

370. Mahadevia, Kanksha and Mayank Vikash, "Climate change-Impact on the Sunderbans: A case Study", ***International Scientific Journal Environmental Science,*** [Online: web] Accessed 7 July 2015 URL: http://environment.scientific-journal.com/articles/2/1.pdf.

371. "Royal Bengal Tiger is vanishing forever", [Online: web] Accessed 30 July 2015 URL:https://poplu.wordpress.com/2009/07/14/royal-bengal-tiger-is-vanishing-forever/.

It is estimated by the expert that the villagers kill an average three tiger every year. Moreover, the concerns are emerging that if this trend of killing of tiger continues then the population of the tiger will be in single digit within one or two years.[372]

Tigers are a highly adaptable species that thrive in right from the snows of Russia to the tropical forests of Indonesia to an isolated refuge of Sundarbans boxed in by humans and the sea.[373] However, another general perception regarding straying of tigers has been linked with the declining fresh water supply to the region encompassing submersion of land due to the sea level rise. The tigers often move upward towards land in search of fresh water that leads the tigers to stray resulting into the man-animal conflict. It is believed that tigers in the Indian side of Sundarbans die because of the intense increase in the level of salinity. However, they strive to adapt to these changes. They migrate to the zone of fresh water. Specialists assume that most of the tigers of the Indian Sundarbans have moved towards the Bangladeshi portion.[374]

Figure: 4.3. Glimpse of a Man-Animal Conflict

Source-URL: https://poplu.wordpress.com/2009/07/14/royal-bengal-tiger-is-vanishing-forever/.

372. Ibid.

373. Loucks, Colby et al. (2010), "Sea level rise and tigers: predicted impacts to Bangladesh's Sunderbans mangroves", ***Climatic Change***, 98: 291-298.

374. Royal Bengal Tiger is vanishing forever", [Online: web] Accessed 30 July 2015 URL:https://poplu.wordpress.com/2009/07/14/royal-bengal-tiger-is-vanishing-forever/.

Mc Inter, an American tiger expert, in one of his publications reported five major causes that are posing threat to the tiger's population. Firstly, the rapid climate change impact hampers the natural supply of food to the tigers. Secondly, in Sundarbans, channels are silted. For that reason, natural protection barriers of forests get affected and the tigers move easily into villages and taste the human flesh. Thirdly, owing to the shortages of natural flow of food supply the aged tigers often tend to randomly stray and move into heavily populated zones in search of food. Human and pet animals have been the easiest target for the aged tigers. Fourthly, rising salinity level may be one of the reasons. Fifthly, the carelessness of the forest guards and their nexus with the hunter giving them chance to hunt freely and frequently leads to this situation. The soundness of the mangrove is destroying and the population of the tigers are getting scattered. This situation often forces them to drive away from this zone. They may come out from their habitats to take retribution.[375]

4.2.3. Human Settlement

Human settlement is another area of concern that is facing the terrible brunt of climate change. Population of Sundarbans is increasing in an unbridled manner worsening further the complex situation day by day. Since most of the islands in the Sundarbans are low-lying, and even the main land does not have any sharp elevation near the front of the sea, any rise in sea level will have direct impact on the land affecting human settlement. There exists a constant battle between human and the sea to stymie the large measures of land being dragged away.

Climate change induced sea level rise has two kinds of impact. The first impact is that land is lost to the sea and landholding is drastically decreasing, asserting more pressure on the agriculture on ever-smaller landholdings. Moreover, the second impact is that the land lost to the

---

375. Ibid.

sea is complicated to reclaim for the purpose of cultivation because the salinity devastates the productivity of the soil.[376]

Sea level is rising more or less throughout the Sundarbans. This rate is approaching 3.14 mm per year near the Sagar Islands and that it could increase to 3.5 mm per year over the next few decades. Due to the large-scale deltaic subsidence, the rate of increase at Bangladesh is more than double.[377] Over a foot and a half rise in sea level would indeed inundate the large parts of the Sundarbans.[378] Coastal communities around the world are the most victim of this sea level rise. This has created mass level dislocation of the population making them 'environmental refugees.'[379]

Due to these scenarios, thousands of people in both India and Bangladesh would be affected and forced to leave their origin home to take refuge elsewhere. It is reported that in the past two decades, four[380] islands in the Sundarbans namely Bedford, Lohachara, Kabasgadi, and Suparibhaga have been permanently inundated rendering thousands of people homeless. It is estimated that 6,000[381] families have been made homeless and became climate refugee. Moreover, it is assessed that approximately 7,000 people have been displaced in the past 30 years from their original homes directly as a consequences of increase in the sea level, coastal erosion, coastal inundation and cyclonic events;

376. WWF Report India (2010), "Sundarbans: Future Imperfect- Climate Adaptation Report", pp.1-28.

377. Hazra et al. (2002), "Sea Level and associated changes in the Sunderbans", ***Science and Culture,*** vol.68, no 9-12, pp.309-321.

378. WWF Report India (2010), "Sundarbans: Future Imperfect- Climate Adaptation Report", pp.1-28.

379. Hazra et al. (2002), "Sea Level and associated changes in the Sunderbans", ***Science and Culture,*** vol.68, no 9-12, pp.309-321.

380. WWF Report India (2010), "Sundarbans: Future Imperfect- Climate Adaptation Report", pp.1-28.

381. Ibid.

these changes have made 1.35 million people's life vulnerable in the Sundarbans.[382]

It is imperative to make out the extent of land loss in Sundarbans to gauge the ground reality. The most vulnerable islands in the southern Indian Sundarbans – Dakshin Surendranagar, Sagar, Namkhana, Moushuni, Lothian, Ghoramara, Dulibhasani, Dhanchi, Dalhousie, Bulchery, Ajmalmari West, Ajmalmari East, Bhangaduni, and Jambudwip are reported to have lost 97.16 sq.km of land.[383] The Sagar Island is reported to have net loss of 30 sq. km area over the past 30 years. The intense assessment of possible dislocation of entire population or loss of original habitat is heightened in the villages of Khasimara, Baisnabpara, Khasimara Char and Baghpara and may seek refuge in the nearby island of Sagar.[384] In the Indian Sundarbans, the net land lost stood 44.042 sq. km/year, an area that is almost identical to 45 football grounds.[385]

In addition to the problems posed by the sea level rise, recurrent coastal flooding, the increased intensity of extreme weather events also poses the big challenges to the security of the human settlements. The constant erosion and failure of the embankments that are built to prevent the seawater invading the islands is another problem throughout the Sundarbans. These problems can be termed as 'rapid onset' kind of environmental disaster.[386] The ideas for embankments

---

382. Danda, Anamitra Anurag and Gayathri Srikanthan (2011), "Indian Sundarbans Delta: A Vision", ***WWF Policy Document Indi,*** p.1-40.

383. WWF Report India (2010), "Sundarbans: Future Imperfect- Climate Adaptation Report", pp.1-28.

384. Hazra et al. (2002), "Sea Level and associated changes in the Sunderbans", ***Science and Culture,*** vol.68, no 9-12, pp.309-321.

385. Center for Science and Environment (2012), "Living with changing climate: Impact, vulnerability and adaptation challenges in Indian Sundarbans".

386. Hazra et al. (2002), "Sea Level and associated changes in the Sunderbans", ***Science and Culture,*** vol.68, no. 9-12, pp.309-321.

were given by Danial Hamilton,[387] a Scottish businessman and these embankments were constructed to halt the saline water at the edges of the coast and to protect the productivity of agricultural land, loss of crop and saline water flooding.

Majority of the embankments were built during 1873 and 1939.[388] An earthen embankment of 3520 km. in length was built. Nevertheless with time, the embankment built gradually eroded away and due to the siltation process the river beds have raised. This has submerged already low placed islands in the Sundarbans. The continued erosion of the embankments has been incurring incremental cost towards its proper maintenance. Over the last two decades, the crop and forest property worth Rupees 950 million squandered and over 0.4 million people have been affected.[389] The intimidation in future owing to these changes will continue to be lingered. The Islands of Ghoramara, Dublat G.P. of Sagar Island, G-Plot and Mousuni are highly susceptible in this regard.[390]

4.2.4. Resource Dependent Livelihood

As discussed in the preceding chapters, the Sundarbans has a plethora of natural resources that provide the livelihood opportunities to the inhabitants dependent on it. In the Sundarbans, people's livelihoods are dependent on forest resources. To the large extent, they are engaged in collection of fish, fuel wood, crabs, golpata, waxes and honey. However, after the agriculture, fisheries are the dominant productive activity providing employment to the large section of the people in this region. Another, resource dependent livelihood such as, honey collection by Mawalis and Golpata collection by the Bawalis is also

387. Center for Science and Environment (2012), "Living with changing climate: Impact, vulnerability and adaptation challenges in Indian Sundarbans".

388. Ibid.

389. Hazra et al. (2002), "Sea Level and associated changes in the Sunderbans", ***Science and Culture,*** vol.68, no. 9-12, pp.309-321.

390. Ibid.

very famous in this region that has been very challenging given the inhospitable and inaccessible forest in which they are found. About 0.74 million people are directly engaged in the livelihood relied on the Sundarbans' resources.[391]

Nearly 42% of the population in the Indian Sundarbans belongs to the scheduled caste and tribes communities. Most of them have been engaged in fishing. The study shows that in Bangladesh between US $351 and $750 per year were earned by about 90% collectors. In the Indian part of Sundarbans, about 90% of people are involved in agriculture and fishing, crab collection or honey collection.[392]

The onset of climate change began to have its negative impact on the forests of the Sundarbans. It exacerbated the existing resources, which is already facing the brunt of man-made activities like over-exploitation of forest resources. There is a consistent declining trend in the fish catch in this region. It is regarded that the change in the level of salinity and the alteration of water flow upstream is the major cause in the decline of the fish catch. In addition to this, over-exploitation of the fishery resources has also been a reason. The heavy mechanized trawlers are penetrating deep into the sea exploiting the fish resources. This led to the reduction in the fish catch directly affecting the local population, which is genuinely dependent on the fish catch alone. In the Sundarbans, the data of catch per unit effort for the last 15 years has showed an overall negative trend with reduction in the major catch Hilsa. The unsustainability of these resources in the near future with onset of climate change will be observed. It is expected that this may endanger the livelihood of the fishermen community in the near future.[393]

---

391. Uddin, Md.Shams et al. (2013), "Climate change impacts on the Sunderbans mangrove ecosystem services and dependent livelihoods in Bangladesh", Asian Journal of Conservation Biology, Vol.2, No. 2, pp.152-156.

392. Hazra et al. (2002), "Sea Level and associated changes in the Sunderbans", ***Science and Culture,*** vol.68, no. 9-12, pp.309-321.

393. Ibid.

The climate change will have its straight impact on the forest products related to the provisioning services of the Sundarbans. Due to the climate change impact on the forest products, occupations related to the forest like honey collection, Golpata collection, income level and seasonality would be severely affected.[394]

4.2.4.1. Conflict between resources and livelihood

As is apparent, the euphonious ecosystem services of the Sundarbans are the lifeline for the inhabitants and the source of their subsistence. The entire livelihood pattern revolves around the forest resources of the Sundarbans. It is mentioned in the above section that massive anthropogenic activities are also responsible for the reduction in the forest. The impact of climate change has been observed to be adding fuel to the fire. The fast and constant depleting forest resource is posing threat on the livelihood patterns of the people of the Sundarbans. There is a growing possibility that this depletion of natural forest resources on which the livelihoods of people depend will culminate into conflict among the people, and between the resources and the livelihoods. With the impact of climate change, the scenario in the Sundarbans will largely be exacerbated by the mammoth displacement and livelihood deprivation due to the forest degradation.

The consistent coastal erosion, embankment failure, frequent inundation of land, the rapid and intense occurrence of the extreme weather events have induced the large scale migration of the people in this region. People are increasingly becoming environmental refugee taking refuge in the adjacent swathes. It has been a common perception among the inhabitants of the Sundarbans that they prefer to live where the food is.[395] This statement is somewhat related to the scale of poverty

394. Uddin, Md.Shams et al. (2013), "Climate change impacts on the Sunderbans mangrove ecosystem services and dependent livelihoods in Bangladesh", Asian Journal of Conservation Biology, Vol.2, No. 2, pp.152-156.

395. WWF Report India (2010), "Sundarbans: Future Imperfect- Climate Adaptation Report", pp.1-28.

where because of the intense poverty the people, they cannot afford to have the luxury of permanent houses. The onslaught of the climate change has made their settlement vulnerable. In these areas, their food requirement depends upon the felicity of the forest resources. The climate change impact seems to be thwarting the people's survival by degrading the natural environment.

The survival of the human and economic well-being is fully contingent on biological diversity that includes all life forms, ecosystem, and ecological processes, acknowledging the hierarchy at genetic, taxa and ecosystem levels. In the Indian Sundarbans, the forest resources, reclaimed areas adjacent to the forest is densely populated and is utilized for the crops, brackish water fisheries, and brick industry as a livelihood.

A constant lacuna between the production of resources and consumption of resources by local population has existed. Though, there is a dearth of the exact and candid data to estimate these issues, however it is evident that the rate of population increase and high dependency on the forest resources will ultimately lead to the shortage of the resources resulting in the over exploitation of mangrove forests. This would definitely create a conflict like situation in the Sundarbans.[396]

Moreover, the constant tension and conflict between conservation and humankind's search for a livelihood has evolved with the increasing population. The process of conservation requires and necessitates the imposition of restriction on the access of the forest and their resources. Nevertheless, the growing needs of the population making them move to encroach into the forest for subsistence, thus seems to be creating another conflict with the administration. The cost of the conservation has been generally high, and the benefits are reaped more globally than

---

396. Mandal, R.N. et al. (2009), "Dwindling Indian Sunderban Mangove: The Way Out", *Sci. & Cult.* 76 (7-8) 275-282.

locally. The forest of the Sundarbans acts as subsistence economy. With no global market for the produce from this tract and little benefits from tourism, a majority of the population is compelled to suffer grinding poverty.[397]

397. Center for Science and Environment (2012), "Living with changing climate: Impact, vulnerability and adaptation challenges in Indian Sundarbans".

CHAPTER FIVE

Implications for India-Bangladesh Relations

This chapter makes an effort to understand the emerging complexities and various dimensions of climate changes in the Sundarbans and their implications on India-Bangladesh relations. India has been wary in the backdrop of the changing phenomena. Some of the critical issues relate to displacement among the inhabitants and the likely creation of refugees and internally displaced people and their crossing of the borders. The spillage of the oil, cross border environmental injuries and the conflicts in the Sundarbans may lead to instabilities on both sides of the border and issues related to bio-piracy, natural resource exploitations, natural and manmade disasters etc.

The tract of Sundarbans sits on both sides of the border of India and Bangladesh. This critical ecological zone has been silently suffering the brunt of climate change. India-Bangladesh relation in the past has witnessed many vicissitudes sometimes leading to very bad patches of relations. On the other hand, these two countries have also shown an extraordinary cooperation and understanding on many issues of bilateral interest.

5.1. Emerging Dynamics of Displacement and Migration

Brown stated that it has been very difficult to find the causative and linear linkages between climate change and forced migration. This is mainly because i) the relationship between climate change and human population is unpredictable; the impact of climate change has been observed differently on various resources of various societies and the capacity to become accustomed to external shocks; ii) the individuals' decision to leave their homes differ widely; it has been highly subjective to decide causality between economic 'pull' and environmental 'push'; and iii) to disaggregate the climate change role from other environmental, economic and social factors needed a serious critical effort into the dark.[398] Nevertheless, the Intergovernmental Panel on Climate Change has reported that the climate change would alone have its greatest impact on migration of human.[399]

Sundarbans does record mass movement both internally and externally, which is a concern for both India and Bangladesh. The onslaught of the climate change has induced large scale problems of migration, and that are often termed as 'Forced migrants,'[400] 'environmental migrants,'[401] 'Crisis migrant,'[402] 'Environmental refugee,'[403] 'climate migrants,' and 'climate refugee.' In both sides of the Sundarbans (India and Bangladesh), people are increasingly becoming internally displaced within their own territorial border due to the climate induced hazards. These displaced people are often called as

398. Brown, Oli (2007), "Climate change and forced migration: Observations, projections and implications", Occasional paper for the ***Human Development Report 2007/2008***, p.6.

399. Ibid.

400. Ibid.

401. Hazra, S. et al. (2002), "Sea level and associated changes in the Sunderbans", ***Science and Culture***, Vol.68, No. 9-12, pp. 309-321.

402. Bose, Sahana (2014), "Illegal migration in the Indian Sunderbans", ***Crisis***, FMR 45.

403. Black, Richard (2001), ***"Environmental Refugees: Myth or Reality?"*** Working Paper No 34, New Issues in

Refugee Research, UNHCR, ISSN 1020-7473. Quoted in Architesh Panda (2010), ***"Climate Refugees: Implications for India"***, Economic & Political weekly, vol.XLV, NO. 20.

This term was firstly introduced by Lester Brown of the World Watch Institute in the 1970s 'internally displaced person' (IDP). However, there are many reasons of being displaced; for instance, Lama has classified displacement into four broad categories especially in the Indian context: i) political causes, encompassing secessionist movements; ii) autonomy movements relating to identity; iii) localized violence and finally; iv) displacement triggered by environmental and development activities.[404] This study deals with environmentally or climate change induced tribulations of population displacement.

The refugee convention of 1951 defines refugee as a person;

"who owing to well-founded fear of being persecuted for reasons of race, religion, nationality, membership of a particular social group or political opinion, is outside the country of his nationality and is unable or, owing to such fear, is unwilling to avail himself of the protection of that country; or who not having a nationality and being outside the country of his former habitual residence as a result of such events, is unable or, owing to such fear, is unwilling to return to it" (Convention Relating to the Rights of Refugees, 1951, art. A.2)[405]

However, there are no internationally agreed definitions of climate refugee. The refugee convention of 1951 does not cover the refugee induced by the environmental degradation or climate change impact. In other words, the issues of climate refugees get a setback from international refugee and immigration policy. However, for the purpose of this study, the definition of 'climate refugee' as elucidated by Biermann and Boas (2009) is adopted.

"People who have to leave their habitats, immediately or in the near future, because of sudden or gradual alterations in their natural environment related to at least one of three impacts of climate change:

---

404. Lama, Mahendra P. (2008), "Internal displacement in India: causes, protection and dilemmas", ***Forced Migration Review,*** 8 pp.24-26.

405. Bommel, Maxime van (2010), ***"Good fences don't make good neighbours: outlining the complexities of protecting climate displaces, with special reference to India and Bangladseh"*** Utrecht University,p.31.

sea-level rise, extreme weather events, and drought and water scarcity" (Biermann & Boas 2009, p.9 cited in Fokemma 2011:20).[406]

Under the purview of this definition, all sorts of climate refugee could be encompassed be it inter-state or intra-state, forced or voluntary, as no distinction has been made (Ibid.20). Moreover, in the course of further research this definition can be contested to accommodate the newer framework.

Lama stated, "The very nature, frequency, depth and dimensions of disasters are expected to undergo drastic changes against the impending backdrop of climate change triggered vulnerabilities."[407] The evolving dimensions of climate refugee and related disasters have been a critical and crucial issue between India and Bangladesh. This new aspects of environmental challenge could make the India-Bangladesh relations much more complex and unconventional particularly in the context of the geo-politics and border management. Moreover, Lama says that disaster and other related calamities are likely to inflict more serious cross border environmental injuries[408] owing to the fact that "eco-systems do not respect national boundaries."[409] The impact of climate change is a problem that requires no permission, no passport, and no military expenditure to hurl injuries. For instance, cyclone Sidr in 2007, Nargis in 2008, Aila in 2009 and Laila in 2010 were the annual extreme weather events among a number of other disasters.[410] Cyclone Aila of

---

406. Fokemma, Syta (2011), "To be or not to be a climate change refugee, that is the question: An interpretive policy analysis of labeling and framing processes of climate change refugee in Bangladesh", Utrecht University.

407. Lama, Mahendra P. (2015), "India and its Neighbours: Policy Priorities for the New Government", a Valedictory address delivered on 25th March 2015 in an International Conference at Centre for South Asian Studies, Jawaharlal Nehru University: New Delhi.

408. Ibid.13.

409. Ibid.14.

410. Musa, A.R.M.A. (2010), "Latest news on climate displacement in Bangladesh: Displacement Solutions", [Online: web] Accessed 7 March 2015, URL: http://displacementsolutions.org/latest-news-on-climate-displacement-in-bangladesh/.

2009 was one of the most dramatic of the climatic disasters to have lately hit the Sundarbans,[411] and that left over 2.3 million people displaced and nearly 8,000 missing between India and Bangladesh.[412]Sundarbans itself was flooded with over 20 ft of water and an estimated 400,000 people were marooned by the flooding.[413] These disasters depicted the intensity of their cross border implications. It is expected that many millions of Bangladeshi would cross over to India in future owing to the rises in sea level that might aggravate further the ongoing dispute between India and Bangladesh over the issues of illegal migration.[414]

Bose argued that in the coming decades the issues of human security would be the prominent agenda item for India and Bangladesh relation.[415] In fact, human insecurity triggered from Bangladesh has always been a major issue in India and Bangladesh relation. To ensure the personal security, human beings migrate to another country, but it creates burden on the resources in the other country that may culminate into the conflict with the people of the receiving country. She argues that environmental crisis and the escalating impacts of climate change in Bangladeshi Sundarbans have become significant causes of the cross-border migration to the region of Indian Sundarbans. She further says that in recent years the land loss and habitats due to the rise in sea level are the two major issues in the regions of Indian Sundarbans. The population of the coastal areas is steadily migrating from one island

411. WWF Report India (2010), "Sundarbans: Future Imperfect- Climate Adaptation Report", p.11.

412. Dhar, Sujoy (2009), ***"Hungry Tides in India's Sunderbans" Aljazeera,*** 14th December. Quoted in Shloka Nath (2011), ***"Environmental Diplomacy: Saving the Sunderbans and Restoring Indo-Bangladesh Friendship"***, Mumbai: Gateway House: Indian Council on Global Relations, p.42.

413. Nath, Shloka (2011), ***"Environmental Diplomacy: Saving the Sunderbans and Restoring Indo-Bangladesh Friendship"***, Mumbai: Gateway House: Indian Council on Global Relations, p.42.

414. Bose, Sahana (2014), "Illegal migration in the Indian Sunderbans", ***Crisis***, FMR 45.

415. Ibid.

to another in the quest for food and shelter. The continual exodus of migrants from Bangladesh into the region of Indian Sundarbans, also termed as 'crisis migrants', often tend to enter illegally into the region of Indian Sundarbans in expectation of an endurance fear in their own country.[416]

Nath (2011) has argued that the Sundarbans could become the epicenter for one of the biggest challenges in the form of "climate change refugee" to face human existence in the coming decades.[417] It is estimated that 70,000 people out of the 4.1 million residing in the Indian part of the Sundarbans islands would become homeless by 2020 because of the climate change induced susceptibilities.[418] The monsoon floods in 1998 in Bangladesh were the worst flooding in the recent memory, and that inundated continually for two months the two-thirds of the country, demolished its agricultural base and infrastructure set up, and made an estimated 21 million people homeless. This disaster led to the fear about long-term future of the country in the context of higher ocean level and more severe cyclonic events.[419]

Bose found two kinds of climate-induced migration in the Sundarbans: i) dwellers of Indian Sundarbans steadily migrate one island to another; and ii) rural inhabitants of Bangladesh infiltrate through the porous border into the Indian side of the Sundarbans. The plight of these Bangladeshi migrants becomes worse as the Government of Bangladesh neither recognizes these people as its own

---

416. Ibid.

417. Nath, Shloka (2011*), "Environmental Diplomacy: Saving the Sunderbans and Restoring Indo-Bangladesh Friendship"*, Mumbai: Gateway House: Indian Council on Global Relations, p.41.

418. Panda, Architesh (2010), "Climate Refugees: Implications for India", ***Economic &Political weekly***, vol.XLV no.20: 76-79.

419. Brown, Oli (2007), "Climate change and forced migration: Observations, projections and implications", Occasional paper for the ***Human Development Report*** 2007/2008.

citizens and nor by India as 'climate refugees.'[420] Bangladesh accuses India of expelling its own Muslim Bengali citizens towards Bangladesh in the name of illegal migrants. On the other, India does not extend them refugee status because this status would create surplus burden on India to provide all round facility to sustain their life. India is not a party to the Refugee Convention of 1951. India refuses to sign this instrument pointing it out as euro-centric. India believes that this instrument is not suitable in relation to the developing world. India further asserts that this instrument primarily was prepared to tackle with the individual cases and not with the cases of large-scale exodus of mass movements. Therefore, this situation worries India because of the anticipated financial burden. It is problematic for India to cater to all refugees from other countries, as it could not meet the all round socio-economic demands of its own millions of people.[421]

The migrants are unnecessarily enmeshed in the orthodox discourse on security and territorial sovereignty between India and Bangladesh. Thus, the blame game begins. The government of Bangladesh does not preclude the migrants' flow from its territory and does not take back those who have been identified as illegal migrants. Bose (2014) observes that such kind of forced migration from Bangladesh symbolizes the breakdown of official adaptation to climate change.[422] It seems so because in Bangladesh, issues relating to migration have not even been mainstreamed with the environmental, disaster management and policy regarding climate change. Thus, no concrete policy pertaining to climate refugee exists.[423] There is however third category of climate

---

420. Bose, Sahana (2014), "Illegal migration in the Indian Sunderbans", *Crisis*, FMR 45.

421. Bommel, Maxine van (2010), ***Good fences don't make good neighbours: Outlining the complexities of protecting climate displaces, with special reference to India and Bangladesh"***, Utrecht University, p.32.

422. Bose, Sahana (2014), "Illegal migration in the Indian Sunderbans", *Crisis*, FMR 45.

423. Ibid.

refugees who also migrate from the Bangladeshi side of Sundarbans to other upward areas of Bangladesh. For instance, Nath has stated that due to the submergence of many islands in the Sundarbans such as Bedford, Lohachara, Kabasgadi, and Suparibhaga; many families were forced to leave their home and many of them have taken refuge to the slums of Dhaka.[424]

The low-lying islands are the most victims of climate change triggered vulnerabilities. The entire region of Sundarbans including the whole of Bangladesh is low-lying land. The rising waves of the sea will wreak havoc in the future. The intensity and severity of destruction is likely to increase. In the last few years, the advent of the climate-induced susceptibilities has posed threats to the very existence of the Sundarbans islands.

The residents of the Carteret Islands, which is a part of Papua New Guinea are likely to be the world's 'first climate change refugee'[425] as the impending dangers of rising seas force them to leave their homes. This tiny island has experienced the first hand consequence of global warming induced sea level rise. In 2005, officially it was decided to abandon this Island, and to relocate the people to the island of Bougainville, 100 km away.[426] This island was a home to 2500 people. Scientists expect that low-lying islands in the Pacific will face the worst terrible threat due to rising seas.[427] The second incidences of relocation

424. Nath, Shloka (2011*), "Environmental Diplomacy: Saving the Sunderbans and Restoring Indo-Bangladesh Friendship"*, Mumbai: Gateway House: Indian Council on Global Relations, p.42.

425. Eckels, H. J. (2008), "Climate change refugees forced to leave Carteret Islands", ***Digital Journal.*** [Online: web] Accessed 7 March 2015 URL: http://www.digitaljournal.com/article/248946.

426. Brown, Oli (2007), "Climate change and forced migration: Observations, projections and implications", Occasional paper for the Human Development Report 2007/2008.

427. Eckels, H. J. (2008), "Climate change refugees forced to leave Carteret Islands", ***Digital Journal.*** [Online: web] Accessed 7 March 2015 URL: http://www.digitaljournal.com/article/248946.

due to the rising sea took place at the Lateau, on the island of Tegua on Vanuatu, where a group of hundred residents was relocated in farther inlands.[428] The third incidence occurred north of the Bering Strait at the Shismaref village that sits on Sarichef Island. The melting permafrost[429] and erosion of seashore altogether have impelled the residents of this island to relocate their village several kilometers to the south.[430]

Alam (2003) argued that at present, Bangladesh is facing land and water crisis, fast growth in population, environmental change and unequal resource distribution. These cases are likely to worsen the prevailing situation in Bangladesh, thus may lead to the large-scale cross-border migration of Bangladeshi people to India at a faster rate.[431] The people of Bangladesh take refuge in India as an easy destination because of many reasons.[432]

i) Under the Indian Constitution, issues of immigration is a subject of central consideration and the whole process of determining immigration whether it is cross-border immigration, or difficult or easy, rests in the hands of the state. This situation often makes the journey towards India an easier one for the Bangladeshis.

ii) The cutoff date for erstwhile Pakistani migrants has also been one of the reasons. July 8th, 1948 was fixed for the rest of the country however, for Assam it was 25th March 1971. Whoever came till1971 were regarded as citizens of the Indian state. Those who came after 1971 attempted to mingle with the mainstream

428. Brown, Oli (2007), "Climate change and forced migration: Observations, projections and implications", Occasional paper for the Human Development Report 2007/2008.

429. It is a thick layer of soil, a subsurface, which exists below freezing point entire the year transpiring mainly in polar regions.

430. Ibid.

431. Alam, Sarfaraz (2003), "Environmentally Induced Migration from Bangladesh to India", ***Strategic Analysis***, Vol.27, No.3.

432. Kamar, Chirantan (2009), "Migration and Refugee issue between India and Bangladesh", ***Scholar's Voice: A New Way of Thinking***, Vol.1, No.1, pp.73-74.

population-creating ambience of confusion. It became very difficult to ascertain the illegal people from Bangladesh. Thus, migrants taking advantages of this situation come to Assam or its adjacent states without any hesitation.

iii) Politicization of this issue has also enhanced to this problem.

iv) In India, to deal with all kinds of immigrants, Foreigners Act 1946 exists. However, in Assam another law, Illegal Migrants (Determination by Tribunals) Act (IMDT) existed that was supposed to protect the illegal migrants masquerading that these people are minority. Thus, this law gave the cozy atmosphere to the migrants from Bangladesh. However, on July 14 2005, Supreme Court of India quashed this law.

v) Owing to similar culture, linguistic and physical attributes, migration throughout the border is a common phenomenon and became an easier practice. More importantly, India grants asylum to the non-Muslim Bangladeshis during the time of communal clash.

vi) The secular and democratic fabric of India often makes them fascinated to cross over the Indian border.

vii) The geographical propinquity and cultural and historical linkages also provide a ground for such migratory trends.

In addition to this, better health care facility, employment also lure the people of Bangladesh to take refuge in India.

An estimate concluded that by 2100, around 120 million people could be made homeless due to the rise in the sea level both in India and Bangladesh and the propinquity of Bangladesh to India will facilitate more people migrating into Indian cities that are already under tremendous pressure in terms of physical and social infrastructures.[433]

433. Rajan, Chella S. (2008), ***"Blue Alert",*** Greenpeace India Society. Quoted in Architesh Panda (2010), "Climate refugee: Implications for India", ***Economic & Political Weekly***, Vol.XLV, No. 20. pp. 76-79.

Myers surmised that climate refugees from Bangladesh might solely exceed all contemporary refugees worldwide and expected that from Bangladesh 26 million refugees will come.[434] A survey conducted in the Khulna district affected from Aila revealed that there was a huge population displacement due to the coastal water logging. As a result, approximately 106,000 people were displaced; people affected from these phenomena migrated to safer places, dry places and other distant districts and in some cases, even to India.[435] Akhter stated that environmentally displaced persons in Bangladesh owing to the impact of disasters like Floods and Cyclone Sidr, which struck Bangladesh in 2007, are not only becoming homeless, but their sources of living on which they subsist, are also getting threatened and these vicissitudes make these people economically susceptible, leading to the augmented poverty and insecurity.[436]

Figure: 5.1. Cyclone caused water logging in coastal area, Khulna, 2009.

Source- Akhtar (2009)

---

434. Panda, Architesh (2010), "Climate refugee: Implications for India", ***Economic & Political Weekly***, Vol.XLV, No. 20. pp. 76-79.

435. Kushol, R. et al. (2009), "Cyclone ***Aila, Initial Assessment Report, with focus on Khulna district***" Unnayan Onneshan, Humanity Watch and Nijera Kori, Dhaka. Quoted in Tahera Akhter (2009), "Climate Change and Flow of Environmental Displacement in Bangladesh", ***Unnayan Onneshan: The Innovators***. pp.1-15.

436. Akhter, Tahera (2009), "Climate Change and Flow of Environmental Displacement in Bangladesh", ***Unnayan Onneshan: The Innovators***. pp.1-15.

Regarding the future predicament of climate refugees, various reports based on various climate models have been published. A report stated that one-meter increase in the level of sea is expected to put approximately 7.1 million people out of place in India, and about 5,764 sq km of land swathes will be eroded away, and 4,200 km of roads as well.[437] Another migratory climate study projects that as the world warms, the rainfall will be concentrated in a shorter period, throwing up a ravaging combination of intense floods and longer periods of drought. If the level of sea rises by up to 1 meter this century, the repercussion would be catastrophic because as many as 10 to 30 million Bangladeshis along the southern coast could be rendered climate refugees[438]. Myers argues, "when global warming takes hold; there could be as many as 200 million people overtaken by the disruptions of monsoon systems and other rainfall regimes, by droughts of unprecedented severity and duration, and by rises in the level of sea and by the events of coastal flooding."[439] Brown (2007) estimated that by 2050 "one in every forty-five people" in the world would have been displaced by climate change.[440]

---

437. National Communication (NATCOM) (2004), Chapter 3: ***"Vulnerability Assessment and Adaptation",*** India's Initial National Communication to the UNFCCC, Ministry of Environment and Forests, Government of India. Quoted in Shloka Nath (2011***), "Environmental Diplomacy: Saving the Sunderbans and Restoring Indo-Bangladesh Friendship"***, Mumbai: Gateway House: Indian Council on Global Relations, pp.1-67. Also Quoted in Architesh Panda (2010), "Climate Refugees: Implications for India"***, Economic &Political Weekly***, vol.XLV no.20: pp. 76-79.

438. Belt, Don (2011), "The coming Storm"***, The National Geographic***, May 2011. Qouted in Nath, Shloka (2011***), "Environmental Diplomacy: Saving the Sunderbans and Restoring Indo-Bangladesh Friendship"***, Mumbai: Gateway House: Indian Council on Global Relations, pp.1-67.

439. Brown, Oli (2007), "Climate change and forced migration: Observations, projections and implications", Occasional paper for the ***Human Development Report*** 2007/2008.

440. Ibid.

Figure: 5.2. Inundated: Aila-hit Canning, a gateway to the Sundarbans
Source- URL: http://www.telegraphindia.com/1130623/images/2306flood_aila1.jpg.

The problem of refugees has become one of the most pressing issues in the India-Bangladesh relations. Zahan (2008) depicted that if this increasing trends of environmental refugees continue, then a country like Bangladesh will not be able to accommodate such a huge uprooted people in near future.[441] Brown (2007) stated that 20 million Bangladeshi people migrate annually to India.[442]

It is stated that in 2001, the Union Home Minister said that over 12 million illegal Bangladeshi immigrants were residing in 17 states of India.[443] Nevertheless, this statement was turned down by Ministry of Home Affairs, Govt. of India as baseless and hearsay. However, another reference showed that the number of illegal immigrants from

---

441. Zahan, Nushrat (2008), "Environmental Security: Coping with climate security of Bangladesh", ***Issue Brief, Bangladesh Institute of Peace and Security Studies***, Issue 3, pp.1-8.

442. Brown, Oli (2007), "Climate change and forced migration: Observations, projections and implications", Occasional paper for the ***Human Development Report*** 2007/2008.

443. Nath, Shloka (2011), ***"Environmental Diplomacy: Saving the Sunderbans and Restoring Indo-Bangladesh Friendship"***, Mumbai: Gateway House: Indian Council on Global Relations, pp.1-67.

Bangladesh in India was 1.2 crore on December 31, 2001.[444] Again in 2001, a report by the Task Force on Border Mangement led by Madhav Godbole kept the figure of illegal immigrants from Bangladesh at15 million, with estimation of around 300,000 entering India every month illegally.[445]Prakash Jaiswal, Minister of State for Home Affairs, in 2004, reported to the Rajya Sabha that the number of illegal Bangladeshis were 1,20,53,950 in India.[446] According to these figures, the number for Assam was 5 million, West Bengal 5.7 million, followed by Bihar at 4.7 million and Delhi at 3.75 million.[447]

Figure: 5.3. Climate refugees from the cyclone hit Sundarbans portraying banner Source-URL:http://www.greenpeace.org/india/Global/india/image/2009/7/climate-refugees-sunderbans-portraits.jpg.

Kumar (2009) pointed out that the Home Minister of India, L.K. Advani mentioned 20 million as the total of illegal immigrants from

444. Rajagopal, Krishnadas (2015), "Centre, Assam delaying border fencing: SC", ***The Hindu***, Delhi, 14 May 2015.

445. Deka, Dr. Kaustubh (2014), "Bengali Muslims who migrated to Assam in 1871 are not 'illegal Bangladeshis'

Migration Debate [Online: web] URL:http://scroll.in/article/748027/unravelling-the-mysteries-of-sleep-how-the-brain-sees-dreams.

446. Ibid.

447. Ibid.

Bangladesh who needed to be sent back. In addition to this, while trying to implement the process of deportation, lot of security forces deployed to resolve the dispute over migrants at the border resulted into the large-scale diplomatic line between the two countries. India asserted that migrants could not have the right to stay permanently in India, whereas Bangladesh alleged India of driving out its own Bengali speaking Muslim citizens on the pretention of Bangladeshi migrants.[448] In 2003, the Foreign Minister of Bangladesh was quoted as saying that "not a single unauthorized Bangladeshi resided in India."[449] Abdul Kalam Azad, a research fellow at the BIISS, said that migration question from Bangladesh to India has become one of the most heated subjects of discussion in Bangladesh because Bangladeshis consider that people are not making their way to India.[450]

These kinds of statements from Bangladesh do indicate that in case the exodus of environmental refugees actually takes place in the aftermath of the effect of climate change in regions like that of Bangladeshi Sundarbans, this could lead to serious diplomatic tussle and possibility of conflict could remain very high between these two countries. Alam (2003) elucidated that the conflict may arise owing to the process of interaction of resource capture (i.e. economic marginalization) and spatial (i.e. ecological) marginalization in any society.[451]

---

448. Kumar, Chirantan (2009), "Migration and Refugee issues between India and Bangladesh", ***Scholars Voice: A New Way of Thinking,*** Vol.1, No.1, pp.64-89.

449. Nath, Shloka (2011***), "Environmental Diplomacy: Saving the Sunderbans and Restoring Indo-Bangladesh Friendship"***, Mumbai: Gateway House: Indian Council on Global Relations, pp.1-67.

450. Friedman, L. (2009), "How will climate refugees impact national security? The border between Bangladesh and India may offer a preview of how climate change could destabilize national", [Online: web] Accessed 7 March 2015 URL: http://www.scientificamerican.com/article/climage-refugees-national-security/.

451. Alam, Sarfaraz (2003), "Environmentally Induced Migration from Bangladesh to India", ***Strategic Analysis***, Vol.27, No.3.

Swain (1996)[452] candidly argued that the paucity of any optimism of survival in other parts of their own country has made people option less but to cross the porous border and to enter into India. A report in the *Far Eastern Economic Review* referred that the southwestern Bangladesh is the main source for people to enter India illegally through the border of West Bengal. There is widespread consensus among the academic community and media personnel that the Southern part of Bangladesh is the fountain of migrants to India. Chief Minister of Assam, P.K. Mahanta, stated that people from Khulna arrive in huge numbers in his state after crossing the border of West Bengal. It has been very hard for the country like Bangladesh, an Islamic state to believe migration of Muslims into the Hindu dominated state of India. It is because the very foundation of Bangladesh is contingent on the idea of Islam.[453]

The population of the Khulna division has declined dramatically whereas the population of adjacent eight border districts of West Bengal increased at the rate of 2.7% while in the rest of the country it was only 1.9% as per the Indian census of India 1981. Simultaneously, at least two million Muslim people found to be disappeared from the Bangladeshi's government census. The number of passports that issued to the people of the Khulna division is also relatively far less than in other parts. This obviously denotes the illegal moods of migration.[454]

5.2. Border Fencing

India and Bangladesh are two distinct sovereign and independent countries where both strive to safeguard their individual national interest and national security. Each country ensures the safety of its

452. Swain, Ashok (1996), "Displacing the Conflict: Environmental Destruction in Bangladesh and Ethnic Conflicts in India", ***Journal of Peace Research***, Vol.33, No.2, pp.189-204.

453. Ibid.194.

454. Ibid.194.

people and territorial boundary from any sort of aggression. India has been keen to have a safe border on the Eastern region mainly with Bangladesh, Bhutan, China, Myanmar and Nepal. India-Bangladesh borders are manned by Border Security Forces (BSF). However, given the huge length of the border, India's largest share of its international border with Bangladesh 4,095.7 kilometer, it has not been possible for the security forces to keep the state protected without proper fencing. The illegal migration from Bangladesh has been a high politics agenda in some of the North East states of India. This is mainly because this has generated host of destabilizing social, political, ethnic and communal tensions and violence within the Indian states. For instance, the sporadic conflict in Assam between the illegal immigrants of Bangladesh and ethnic communities within the state has been widely recorded (Routrey 2008; Bhaumik 2010; cited in Bommel 2010).

Figure: 5.4. Fence along the India-Bangladesh Border

Source- URL:http://www.telegraphindia.com/1110724/jsp/7days/story_14280419.jsp.

India began to fence its international border with Bangladesh since mid 1980s. The states of West Bengal (2,216.7 km), Assam (663 km), Meghalaya (443 km), Tripura (856 km) and Mizoram (318 km) have their common border with Bangladesh.[455] The fencing of the border which started in 1986 till date has completed 2,677.81 km.[456] Another 621 miles cannot be fenced but patrolled because it runs across the delta's shifting rivers.[457] This fence is longer even than taking all together the 'border fence of US-Mexico, the Israel-Palestine wall and the old Berlin wall.'[458] This fence is an 8-foot high built with double-walled and barbed wire. Both government of India and Bangladesh have regarded to a 150 yards "no man's-land" on both sides of the border. This is because many of the houses have a front door in one country and a back door in the other.[459] However, the Indian government has chosen deliberately not to declare its borderland area as "no man's land," because its citizens privatively own the entire area on the border side. If India declares so, it would be bound to acquire the fenced private land and compensate landowners.[460]

Moreover, the fencing of the border has also generated some serious problems within the Indian side. The fencing issue becomes more important now against the backdrop of climate change triggered likely displacement of many millions of Bangladeshis. Fencing may prevent the intrusion into the Indian border. However, it is also likely

---

455. Prakash, A. and Shailja Menon (2011), "Fenced Indians Pay for 'Security'", ***Economic & Political weekly***, Vol.XLVI, No.12, pp.33-37.

456. Ibid.

457. Banerjee, Bidisha (2010), "The Great Wall of India", ***Slate***, 20 December 2010. [Online: web] Accessed 12 March 2015 URL: http://www.slate.com/articles/health_and_science/green_room/2010/12/the_great_wall_of_india.html.

458. Hussain, D. (2009), "Fencing off Bangladesh: India's 2500-mile border fence is meant to keep out smugglers, but simply living on the boundary is a dangerous business", [Online: web] Accessed 7 March 2015 URL: http://www.theguardian.com/commentisfree/2009/sep/05/bangladesh-india-border-fence.

459. Banerjee, Bidisha (2010), "The Great Wall of India", ***Slate***, 20 December 2010. [Online: web] Accessed 12 March 2015 URL: http://www.slate.com/articles/health_and_science/green_room/2010/12/the_great_wall_of_india.html.

460. Prakash, A. and Shailja Menon (2011), "Fenced Indians Pay for 'Security", ***Economic & Political weekly***, Vol.XLVI, No.12, pp.33-37.

to be widely resented on the Bangladeshi side. An environmental commentator based in London, Isabel Hilton, argued, "Bangladesh is such kind of a country that could generate more climate refugees than anywhere else on the earth."[461] For Hilton, fence imparts a clear message that wherever climate change induced refugees in Bangladesh are going to go, they are not supposed to go to India.[462] A. K. Singh, a retired Air Marshal of Indian Air Force, expressed that some of the refugees might be imbibed by India if one-third of Bangladesh is inundated, but not all.[463] India regards the coastal flooding of the low-lying area a national security issue.[464]

The purpose to build fence, as India maintains, is to defend the country against smuggling, terrorism and infiltration into the country.[465] However, Francois Gemenne argued, "for countries that build fences, it's not really a way to control immigration but a way to reassure the electorate; they are more symbolic than really an effective immigration tool."[466] Nevertheless, the statement made by Francois Gemenne may be contradicted. If fences are not the way to control immigration effectively, then what other mechanism should be in place. Moreover, fences stood for the protection of the masses of the state concerned. Given the overall security scenario, the protection of

---

461. Friedman, L., (2009), "How will climate refugees impact national security? The border between Bangladesh and India may offer a preview of how climate change could destabilize national". [Online: web] Accessed 7 march 2015 URL: http://www.scientificamerican.com/article/climage-refugees-national-security/.

462. Ibid.

463. Ibid.

464. Ibid.

465. Banerjee, Bidisha (2010), "The Great Wall of India", ***Slate***, 20 December 2010. [Online: web] Accessed 12 March 2015 URL: http://www.slate.com/articles/health_and_science/green_room/2010/12/the_great_wall_of_india.html.

466. Friedman, L., (2009), "How will climate refugees impact national security? The border between Bangladesh and India may offer a preview of how climate change could destabilize national". [Online: web] Accessed 7 march 2015 URL: http://www.scientificamerican.com/article/climage-refugees-national-security/.

the border should be an essential agenda along with the welfare of the border communities of a country concerned.

Paskal while stating that prospects of large-scale migration from Bangladesh represent a real threat to India asserted, "There are many countries that would like to see India a weakened state, like China and Pakistan; if Bangladesh gets destabilized by climate change, the radical Islamist forces over there are likely to hit the vulnerable communities with pace, and often it may culminate into the deadly attack like the one in Mumbai in 2008."[467]

Banerjee (2010) argued that the advent of climate change might force many millions of Bangladeshi people from their homes; the fence will act as a hindrance for many of them to take refuge in India. Accelerating climate change will further enhance the cross-border tension due to the fenced border. Therefore, she suggested that instead of increasing the length of the fence, it would be better for India to give up its Great Wall as a matter of symbolism and pragmatism.[468]

Bangladeshi academic, Imtiaz Ahmed opined, "The Great Wall of China could not withstand Mongol invaders and was finally given up; the Berlin Wall collapsed; thereby, this Great Wall of India, a fence of billion-dollars, fate of which seems even more tenuous and children can snip it through with twenty-cent scissors."[469] Bommel (2010) argued that the way the large scale of Bangladeshi migrants have come frequently in conflict with Indian population, especially in Assam, the India's response to these developments is rather sadly relatively justifiable.[470] A Member of Parliament, Sirajuddin Ajamal, exhorted

467. Ibid.

468. Banerjee, Bidisha (2010), "The Great Wall of India", ***Slate***, 20 December 2010. [Online: web] Accessed 12 March 2015 URL: http://www.slate.com/articles/health_and_science/green_room/2010/12/the_great_wall_of_india.html.

469. Ibid.

470. Bommel, Maxime van (2010), ***"Good fences don't make good neighbours: outlining the complexities of protecting climate displaces, with special reference to India and Bangladesh"*** Utrecht University.

the government to build a concrete wall around Bangladesh. Because of the influx of Bangladeshi migrants, the Indian Muslims of Assam had suffered a lot over the years as they had been tagged as Bangladeshis.[471]

The Supreme Court of India recently slammed the Central government of India and Government of Assam for making delay in fencing of the eastern border. The apex court accused the Centre and the Assam of "dragging its feet" on fortifying the eastern 'porous' border with Bangladesh despite its judgment that security chinks are posing serious threat to the lives of the ordinary people. The bench led by Ranjan Gogoi has appointed a court commissioner to unearth the ground realities of happenings on the border to report the court. The court has appointed the senior lawyer Upamanyu Hazarika as a court commissioner to visit the border. The court further questioned the Government's resolve to secure the eastern border even after the 67 years of independence.[472]

5.3. Oil Spills in the Sundarbans

The Sundarbans is the ecologically critical and fragile tract endowed with the mangrove forest. The oil spill in Sundarbans is likely to bring newer disasters in near future. The government of Bangladesh opened up the delta for the commercial vessels in 2011 to sail through the delta. The route is the southern port of Chittagong to the country's Centre. The commercial vessels began to carry everything from oil and cement to food, slashing cost and travel time. The environmental experts have described this decision as a "bomb waiting to explode."[473]

Interdependency between India and Bangladesh is visible in terms

---

471. Gupta, Smita (2015), "Parliament puts seal of approval on LBA", ***The Hindu***, Delhi, 8 May 2015

472. Rajagopal, K. (2015), "Centre, Assam delaying border fencing: SC", ***The Hindu***, Delhi, 14 May 2015.

473. Special correspondent (2014), "Development 'threatens fragile Sunderbans'in Bangladesh", ***The Hindu***, Delhi, 20 December 2014.

of sharing of natural resources such as water, forest etc. Bangladesh retains 57 cross-boundary rivers, of which 54 are shared with India.[474] Any loss in the quality and quantity of shared water upstream in India would definitely affect the parts of Bangladesh. Any damage in one part of the Sundarbans is bound to affect the other parts. The oil spill in Bangladeshi Sundarbans is likely to affect the Indian side of Sundarbans.

Given the ecological importance attached to the river Sela that is home to the rare Irrawady dolphins, the government of Bangladesh declared some areas of Southern Sundarbans a dolphin sanctuary in 2001 after a research report recommended that this area is home to some 6,000 Irrawady dolphins.[475] The navigation through this area was restricted, but Sela River opened for navigation again from January 6, 2015.[476] On December 9, 2014, a cargo ship collided into an oil tanker in the deep fog in Sela River.[477] It is reported that the tanker was en route to supply the oil to a power plant. The vessel however, crashed into the tanker and leaked near about 350,000 litres of furnace oil that spilled in the Sela River in the areas of Bangladeshi Sundarbans.[478] It is reported that spillage of oil spread along 40 km section of the river.[479] The incident of oil spillage in Sela River has caused severe damages to the sustainability of this unique environment. The ecosystem of Sundarbans acts as a buffer against environment disasters emanating

474

475. Pandey, Kundan (2014), "Oil spill in Bangladesh's Sela river threatens dolphin sanctuary", [Online:web] Accessed 10 February 2015 URL: http://www.downtoearth.org.in/content/oil-spill-bangladesh-s-sela-river-threatens-dolphin-sanctuary.

476. Ahmed, Kazimuddin (2015), "Sunderbans oil spill: who will clean the mess?" , [Online: web] Accessed 10 February 2015 URL: http://www.downtoearth.org.in/content/sundarbans-oil-spill-who-will-clean-mess#.VLfv1HPxLqB.

477. Pandey, Kundan (2014), "Oil spill in Bangladesh's Sela river threatens dolphin sanctuary", [Online:web] Accessed 10 February 2015 URL: http://www.downtoearth.org.in/content/oil-spill-bangladesh-s-sela-river-threatens-dolphin-sanctuary.

478. Ibid.

479. Ibid.

from situations like cyclones. Losing this ecosystem will be a big loss for humanity.[480]

The effects of oil spill have become apparent as the fish, crabs and all other wildlife are observed floating dead on the water since happening of the incident.[481] The marine life has been badly threatened. This is an "unprecedented disaster" that could have inherent serious consequences as it hurls grave danger to the whole floral and faunal species of the Sundarbans, be it big or small. Spillage effects would be visible on land and in water, and people residing in the area would also be affected.[482] Ainun Nishat, a leading Hydrologist of Bangladesh and an authority on Sundarbans, opined that it would be very difficult to realize the immediate impacts caused by oil spill and that its impact would be apparent at least five years after when it culminates into the real magnitude of destruction.[483]

Figure: 5.5. Oil Spill in the Sundarbans

Source- westbengaltourism.gov.in

480. Special correspondent (2014), "Development 'threatens fragile Sunderbans'in Bangladesh", ***The Hindu***, Delhi, 20 December 2014

481. .Ibid.

482. Ahmed, Kazimuddin (2015), "Sunderbans oil spill: who will clean the mess?" , [Online: web] Accessed 10 February 2015 URL: http://www.downtoearth.org.in/content/sundarbans-oil-spill-who-will-clean-mess#.VLfv1HPxLqB.

483. Ibid.

The spillage could not remain confined to the tract of Bangladeshi Sundarbans. It even crossed into the Indian Sundarbans that led to the increased panic among the Indian authorities and people. The Indian officials are now getting ready to deal with the possible challenges to the environment in time to come. Pradip Vyas intimated the media persons that wildlife officials have been sent in the area to check the spill spreading to India. Locals in the Indian side of Sundarbans have observed some oil impact in this side of the river. The wildlife in the Sundarbans is paying the most price of the oil spill. Secretary of Sundarbans Matsyajibi Joutha Sangram Committee, a prime body of fishermen in the region, has stated that a large number of fish floating dead in the river have been seen by some fishermen. Furthermore, the movement of sea animals like dolphins and crocodiles across Sela and neighbouring Passur has also been observed to be very little. The environmentalists have further cautioned that the chemical could enhance the delicacy and fragility of the ecology of the Sundarbans.[484]

The widespread voices are emerging within Bangladesh about India acting unfriendly. It is alleged that India has maintained a resounding silence over the spilling issue. The Indian Prime Minister advocated a policy of "neighbour first" at the SAARC forum in November 2014 which actually transpired nearly a fortnight before the spill. Therefore, given this backdrop, many Bangladeshis think that whether India's communiqué of "neighbour first" is because of diplomatic constraints or something else, or does India just not care about what happens to its neighbour.[485]

---

484. Pandey, Kundan (2014), "India on high alert after massive oil spill threatens Sunderbans ecology", [Online: web] Accessed 10 February 2015 URL: http://www.downtoearth.org.in/content/india-high-alert-after-massive-oil-spill-threatens-sunderbans-ecology.

485. Ahmed, Kazimuddin (2015), "Sunderbans oil spill: who will clean the mess?", [Online: web] Accessed 10 February 2015 URL: http://www.downtoearth.org.in/content/sundarbans-oil-spill-who-will-clean-mess#.VLfv1HPxLqB.

Anurag Danda,[486] argued that there are no reasons behind India's silence either politically or diplomatically. He says that given the current ambience of cooperation, at least when India and West Bengal are keen to seal the land boundary agreement for swapping enclaves between India and Bangladesh, this kind of things of deep silence on part of India makes no sense. Danda thinks that the silence is not on the issue of cooperation to clean the mess in the Sundarbans caused by the oil spill. Rather silence seems visible on the lack of proper knowledge and expertise that are needed to grapple with the mess of the spillage of oil in an estuary which is opposed to the open waters, and especially more so in the Sundarbans, a tract full of peculiarities. Danda, furthermore adds that, "I do not think India can do any better in such a situation. It is just that India does not permit river traffic within protected areas. I do not think inaction or even suggestion of collective action is due to political or diplomatic constraints." Vivek Menon at Wildlife Trust of India (WTI) has also said that there is a lack of knowledge to deal with the problem and there exists no specialized unit to deal spillage of oil vis-à-vis ecological ramification in India.[487]

5.4. Thermal Power Plant and Sundarbans Forest

The potentiality of future oil spill could not be denied, especially when, Bangladesh has signed a deal with India to establish a thermal power plant based on coal in Bagerhat district of Bangladesh adjacent to the Sundarbans forest. Thermal Power Plant established at Backergange (Bagerhat) in Bangladesh might create environmental hazards as this set up will release its industrial effluents in chunk will indeed threaten the already delicate ecosystem of Sundarbans ahead. Power plant will be set up in Rampal upzila. The Sundarbans of Bangladesh is a protected area that falls under the purview of the forest department, while 10 km buffer zone around the forests is the onus of the environment

486. Ibid.

487. Ibid.

department. The project site is 4 km away from the buffer zone, which is an ecologically critical portion of the Sundarbans. This project will be spread over 800 hectares, with production capacity of 1,320 MW.[488] This step has led to the massive agitation against project and demanding relocation of the plant.

Experts argue that rapid development in Bangladesh on the doorstep of the ecologically sensitive Sundarbans means "environmental disasters" like the oil spill.[489] The plant is supposed to build on the banks of the Passur River that passes through the forest. Forest officials are concerned about the waste generated from the burnt coal that would be dumped in the river as soon as the plant is commissioned by 2018. Waste and hot water management are the main concerns for the officials. There is a wide consensus that the plant will contaminate the Sundarbans' rivers and emit thick dust, which will reach to the forest. Y.V. Jhala opined that the power plant impact in combination with the enhanced shipping will be "disastrous" and will jeopardize a "whole range of aquatic animals and the Bengal tigers." He further argued that allowing ships to sail through the delta, Bangladesh is playing with conservation of the Sundarbans in order to keep the pace of development. He suggests that Bangladesh should completely ban the shipping through the forest and relocate the plant elsewhere.[490]

488. Juneja, Sugandh (2012), "Sunderbans at risk", [Online: web] Accessed 10 March 2015 URL: http://www.downtoearth.org.in/content/sundarbans-risk.

489. Special correspondent (2014), "Development 'threatens fragile Sunderbans'in Bangladesh", ***The Hindu***, Delhi, 20 December 2014.

490. Ibid.

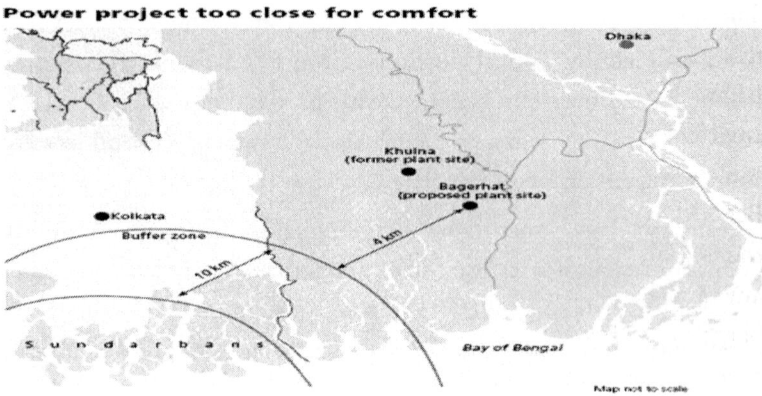

Figure: 5.6. Thermal Power Plant adjacent to the Sundarbans Forest

Source- http://www.downtoearth.org.in/content/sundarbans-risk.

An independent wildlife expert of Bangladesh, Mohsinuzzman Chowdhury, has raised the alarm regarding the sensitivity of the Sundarbans. He said that there is not only increased fear of the pollution coming from the projects but huge numbers of workers who would place higher pressure on the fragile forest. Nowadays, directly or indirectly nearly one million people are contingent on the forest. This number could reach to more than five million in the next coming decade.[491]

The Ramsar convention secretariat, expressing concerns over the exacerbating conditions of the Sundarbans, stated that the joint venture between the Power Development Board of Bangladesh and National Thermal Power Corporation (NTPC) of India could be a potential menace to the Sundarbans.[492] The water necessity for the plant will be replenished by the Passur River. Nevertheless, Syeda Rizwana Hasan says, "The River helps maintain balance of sweet and saline water that needed for the survival of the plant species of the

491. Ibid.

492. Juneja, Sugandh (2012), "Sunderbans at risk", [Online: web] Accessed 10 March 2015 URL: http://www.downtoearth.org.in/content/sundarbans-risk.

Sundarbans."[493] Ronald Halder, a wildlife expert in Dhaka, says that this project will be a major jolt to the communities of Fishermen of Bagerhat because of the presence of many fishing grounds. Senior environmental official argued that any developmental project carries some positive and negative aspects; both districts of Khulna and Bagerhat are virgins with no established industries. Halder states that the Government can shift this project to somewhere else if it wants. In any case, this project near the forest of Sundarbans would not be worth bargaining. If Government still maintains its obstinacy, then it would require thinking again to set up a plant just near the Sundarbans.

5.5. Resuscitation of the Sundarbans: India-Bangladesh Joint Action

India and Bangladesh have been involved in issues other than the climate change. The climate-induced problems never took the center stage in the mainstream politics between India and Bangladesh. A.S. Panneerselvan argued that Sundarbans is not a determining factor towards India's journey to becoming a regional superpower. Issues pertaining to the strategic and economic significance matter a lot for the government. The closer looks on all rounds of political activities of Bangladesh Nationalist Party (BNP) in Bangladesh would be more significant than, say, Sundarbans. He further said that the Sundarbans is not a single case of a myopic vision, however, part of a larger scheme and approach regarding issues, which are not deemed special to India's position in the region.[494]

However, the way newer dimensions of problems are evolving within the Sundarbans, have necessitated for the two governments to step in to save this uniquely fragile ecosystem. The very presence

---

493. Ibid.

494. Ahmed, Kazimuddin (2015), "Sunderbans oil spill: who will clean the mess?" , [Online: web] Accessed 10 February 2015 URL: http://www.downtoearth.org.in/content/sundarbans-oil-spill-who-will-clean-mess#.VLfv1HPxLqB

of this mangrove ecosystem is the best asset and treasure both India and Bangladesh possess that is required to be paid attention. Sugata Hazra has said that climate can affect everyone beyond geographical boundaries.[495] Rising seas have increased the fear of disappearance of the Sundarbans. This can be observed that in the last 25 years five island are reported to have been submerged. The latest one is the New Moore Island, whose submergence is confirmed by Jadavpur University.[496] The New Moore Island has been the issue of contention between India and Bangladesh for a long period now. Every country claimed over its sovereignty. Nevertheless, the brunt of climate change, induced sea level rise, put an end to that contentious issue. This sort of events shows the magnitude of the problems and rather rings a wake-up call for India and Bangladesh. Therefore, adaptation to climate change impacts is another area in the realm of cooperation between India and Bangladesh.[497]

The convergence of governments' action of the two countries relating to the Sundarbans is not unprecedented. However, sensing with problems emerging within the Sundarbans, quite a few joint actions have now been initiated. In 2004, a joint census of tigers was conducted.[498] Later, in January 2010, environment ministers of both countries joined hands to protect the Sundarbans from degradation of environment. Environment and Forest Minister, Jairam Ramesh and his Bangladeshi counterpart Hasan Mahmud in Kolkata launched the joint programme. Ramesh said, "There would be a joint forum between India and Bangladesh for protection of Sundarbans ecosystem that spreads from India to Bangladesh." He further added that the forest

495. Chouhan, Chetan (2010), "India, Bangladesh join hands for Sunderbans", ***Hindustan Times***, New Delhi, 28 March 2010.

496. Ibid.

497. Ibid.

498. Ahmed, Kazimuddin (2015), "Sunderbans oil spill: who will clean the mess?", [Online: web] Accessed 10 February 2015 URL: http :// www.downtoearth.org.in / content /sundarbans –oil –spill –who –will -clean-mess#. VLfv1HPxLqB.

department would work in close coordination to protect and conserve the fragile ecosystem of the Sundarbans.

The India-Bangladesh Eco-system Forum was proposed to be set up in 2010. This forum will involve all non-governmental and civil society organization of both the countries. The main purpose of this forum includes the major coordination efforts in afforestation, management of mangroves and conservation of tiger.[499] This idea has been innovative. The effort is the first of its kind for India in using bilateral environmental problems to foster broader regional cooperation between India and Bangladesh.[500]

Figure: 5.7. Jairam Ramesh with His Bangladeshi Counterpart, Hasan Mahmud in Kolkata on April 4, 2010.
Source-URL: http://photodivision.gov.in/writereaddata/webimages/upload/W-9513l.jpg.

499. India-Bangladesh Sunderbans Ecosystem Forum to be launched [Online: web] URL: http://www.thehindu.com/todays-paper/indiabangladesh-sunderbans-ecosystem-forum-to-be-launched/article744688.ece; The India- Bangladesh Sundarbans Ecosystem Forum to be launched in September [Online: web] URL: http://www.ecosensorium.org/2010/04/india-bangladesh-sundarbans-ecosystem.html.

500. Nath, Shloka (2011), ***"Environmental Diplomacy: Saving the Sunderbans and Restoring Indo-Bangladesh Friendship"***, Mumbai: Gateway House: Indian Council on Global Relations, pp.1-67.

An Integrated Coastal Zone Management project is put in place for the better protection of coastal areas. The Union Government had approved the Rs.1,156 crore for this project, of this Rs.300 crore was fixed to be spent only in West Bengal, most of it on the Sundarbans. This project was funded by the World Bank in order to address the concern of coastal erosion and embankment failure, and to building of storm shelters, promotion of eco-tourism, improving the livelihood condition of the residents of this region and electrification of Sagar Islands. Moreover, 13th Finance Commission of India had sanctioned a grant of Rs.450 crore to strengthen the embankments at all the critical areas in the Sundarbans.[501]

The Prime Ministers of both countries inked a Memorandum of Understanding (MOU) on the conservation of the Sundarbans in 2011.[502] Both the Government of India and the Government of the People's Republic of Bangladesh are the party to the Convention on Biological Diversity 1992. Moreover, these two countries are contracting parties to the Ramsar Convention on Wetlands 1971. These two countries discerning the global importance of the Sundarbans that is recognized as the World Heritage Site and Ramsar site, reached to an above stated MOU in Dhaka on September 6th 2011 in order to monitor and conserve the Sundarbans. The Sundarbans is home to a rich biodiversity comprising huge varieties of rare species of flora and fauna. It plays a very vital role by protecting the mainland from constant flooding, tidal waves and extreme cyclone. The huge ecological significance of the Sundarbans necessitated the urgency to come on the board together to manage this ecosystem jointly.

501. India-Bangladesh Sunderbans Ecosystem Forum to be launched [Online: web] URL: http://www.thehindu.com/todays-paper/indiabangladesh-sunderbans-ecosystem-forum-to-be-launched/article744688.ece.

502. Ministry of External Affairs, Government of India (2011), "MOU between India and Bangladesh on Conservation of the Sunderban", [Online: web] Accessed 27 May 2015 URL: http://mea.gov.in/bilateraldocuments.htm?dtl/5141/MOU+between+India+and+Bangladesh+on+Conservation+of+the+Sundarban.

This MOU consists of eight articles. The article II is related to strategy to conserve the Sundarbans. To exploit the potentiality of the Sundarbans for development and eradication of poverty, both countries agreed to the following points:

1. "consider and adopt appropriate joint management and joint monitoring of resources;
2. explore the possibility of implementing conservation and protection efforts, encourage mangrove regeneration, habitat restoration and rehabilitation programs, which would eventually increase the potential for carbon sequestration;
3. develop a long term strategy for creating ecotourism opportunities for both countries, which will create synergy and generate greater revenue."[503]

The article III is the most vital as it plans to develop strategy for the human beings, their livelihood patterns, deprivation from flooding, and similar other related disasters, man-animal conflict, increasing pollution, and resource depletion. The parties of this agreement observe that the ecosystem of Sundarbans is largely influenced by the human uses of this forest and human settlements around the Sundarbans. Given this situation, both parties agreed to prepare roadmap to have a better relationship between the ecosystem and the human settlements. In addition, both countries will discern the opportunities for livelihood creation in such a way that do not adversely affect the ecosystem of Sundarbans.

The article V of this MOU proposes to carry out research to build a common and shared knowledge of the impacts of climate change. Thereby, an appropriate adaptation strategy could be implemented. Under article VI, both parties are committed to enhance the level of collaboration in order to bolster the management of the Sundarbans.

503. Ibid.

To preclude the smuggling and poaching of wildlife, officials from both sides will exercise patrolling along the respective borders.

The period of this memorandum will be five years, which shall be extended automatically at the end of each period unless it is terminated by the mutual consent of the parties concerned.

The recent spillage in the Sela River of the Sundarbans has largely degraded mangrove ecosystem. This sheer non-climatic anthropogenic disaster became an important area of cooperation between these two countries to overcome the spilling effects. These anthropogenic activities will, definitely bolster the worst impact of climate change on the Sundarbans. Shahab Enam Khan of Jahangirnagar University, Dhaka opined that there should be a collective action between India and Bangladesh to have the better safeguards mechanism for the Sundarbans from a greater management perspective. However, there exists a problem of disjointed policy. As Shahab said, "There persists a major missing component, if we talk about the single landscape narrative of Sundarbans; and that missing component is the lack of synchronization in political and administrative arrangements between the two countries in terms of policy and action. Both countries work with their own sets of policies management frameworks and approaches."[504]

504. Ahmed, Kazimuddin (2015), "Sunderbans oil spill: who will clean the mess?", [Online: web] Accessed 10 February 2015 URL: http://www.downtoearth.org.in/content/sundarbans-oil-spill-who-will-clean-mess#.VLfv1HPxLqB.

Chapter Six

Conclusion

Many scientific studies have corroborated the fact that the climate of the earth is constantly changing over time. Nevertheless, what exactly caused the advent of climate change is widely debated at both the scientific and the political fora. The Intergovernmental Panel on Climate Change (IPCC) 2007 attributed this phenomenon of global warming induced climate change largely to the anthropogenic activities. Some parts of the world, especially low-lying coastal region have been the most adversely affected by this phenomenon. India and Bangladesh have been identified among the 27 countries most vulnerable to the climate change induced accelerated sea level rise.

Nowadays, the issue of climate change has become an important part of the global discourse. There is a visible dearth of unanimity over the question of inception of the phenomenon of climate change. It is strongly believed that human beings have always influenced their environment, and it is only since the incipient of the industrial revolution, mid-18th century that the impacts of man-made activities have begun to traverse globally. R. K. Pachaury has enumerated that the problems of climate change came to the light in 1988 at a time when North America incurred severe drought and an unusually hot summer. Desai in his *Climate Change: economic and historical perspective* has clarified that the issues of climate change were not the case to focus on very long ago. For him, it meant that climate change phenomenon is a recent one. Desai believes that atmospheric scientists were the early movers on the concerns of climate change rather than the activists of the green movement. Desai stipulated that at the political forum, the first two head of the state from the developing world highlighted the matter of climate change at the global level in the 1980s –President Ershad of Bangladesh and President Gayoom of Maldives.

Hence, it is understandable that an enigma of this non-traditional climate change is not new to the scientific world. Rather we can say that these phenomena are new to the political world at a time when its adverse impact was felt socially, economically and politically across the nook and corner of the globe. The impact of climate change has potentiality to destabilize countries like Maldives, Bangladesh, India and Kiribati, and particularly the low-lying countries and islands. The climate change issues have emerged as a core concern in form of non-military and non-traditional security threat respecting no territorial boundary, and requiring no passport and visa to move. With the advent of globalization, after the collapse of the Soviet Union, these issues got pace and attention of the world moved away from the traditional form of security.

The low-lying coastal region like the Sundarbans is highly susceptible to the impact of climate change. The euphonious floral and faunal diversity of the Sundarbans ecosystem makes it unique around the world. By virtue of its dynamic nature, it is often termed "the barometer of change." It is both unique and uniquely fragile. It is unique owing to the existence of one of the most extensive mangrove forest in the world lying in a vast deltaic place where freshwater and seawater mingles; and also because of the presence of an endangered species like Royal Bengal Tiger, and human habitation. It has been ironical that its fragility protrudes from its uniqueness, which remains susceptible to the changes in its ambience due to climate change. Mahadevia and Vikash stated that the Sundarbans being an innocent victim of burgeoning global warming and climate change faces a direct threat to its very existence.

The decreasing freshwater flow from Himalayan rivers predicted for the dry season (dry season getting drier) and gradual increase in sea level the likely enhancement of the severity of salinity ingression in the Sundarbans could be rather very regressive. This has also enhanced the process of coastal erosion jeopardizing the existence of the Sundarbans. Though the process of erosion and accretion have been a natural phenomenon, certain well evident pattern of changes in climate and anthropogenic activities in recent years have added to these natural phenomena aggravating situations in the whole tract of the Sundarbans.

It is rather difficult to attribute the present changes in the Sundarbans directly and wholly to climate change. However, the changes in the Sundarbans are highly perceptible in respect of changes in temperature of sea surface, precipitation pattern, occurrence of extreme weather events, and changes in the sea level. It is observed that eastern coastal region is more vulnerable than the western coastal region. There is a pervasive consensus on the fact that precipitation pattern will be changed in the wake of global warming. The Center for Science and Environment (CSE) stated that the exact nature of this kind of change over Sundarbans is not yet pellucid. On the other hand, WWF India (2010) considers that there has been an agreement over changes in the precipitation pattern over the Sundarbans.

The changes in the frequency of cyclonic activities and its magnitude have turned out to be more disastrous in the climatic patterns of the Sundarbans. A consensus is found among the various researchers on the issue of magnitude of cyclonic activities. They consider that there transpired changes in the local weather; and severity of cyclones have gone up, possibly as a corollary of rising SST.

The rise in the level of sea is another prominent threat for the existence of the Sundarbans. The rising trends of the sea level have jeopardized the future viability of the Sundarbans. That there is lack of unanimity among researcher on the real extent and magnitude of this change in the sea level is clearly apparent. However, an agreement among the researcher on the issue of sea level rise adjoining to the Sundarbans areas can be observed. Like the increase in the sea surface temperature, the rate of relative sea level rise in Sundarbans has also been observed to be higher than the global average rate of sea level rise. This has occurred due to a combination of factors on which the entire dynamics of any delta and coastline depends, namely compaction and tectonic subsidence, relative sea level rise and wave action, and finally supply of sediments from the rivers. The deltaic region of Sundarbans exhibits all the above features. However, the exact reason is not pinpointed in case of sea level rise in an Indian Sundarbans; for the Bangladeshi Sundarbans, the monsoonal rains and land subsidence are found as a major dominant factor.

Climate change induced drivers of change have its profound impact on various aspects of the Sundarbans. These include changes in the mangrove forest cover, biodiversity, wildlife diversity and behavior, changes in the human settlement, embankment failure, effects on resource dependent livelihood. Sea level rise, increasing salinity pattern, constant coastal erosion, flooding and submergence of the island along with the intense extreme weather events have caused massive upheaval in the geography of Sundarbans. The man-made related anthropogenic factors like increasing population, widespread exploitation of natural resources, deforestation, and reclamation have also been responsible to a large extent as it is evident through the various studies on the Sundarbans. The evidences of the onslaught of the climate change induced drivers of change have been found to be adding fuel to fire.

The pattern of salinity inside the forest will change considerably because of climate change. There is a growing consensus among the scholars that intrusion of saline water due to reduction of freshwater flow upstream backed up by the sea level rise has been the major factor for the loss of this euphonious vegetative tract of mangrove forest. This study delineated that the level of saline blanks have grown significantly from 38.93 sq. km to 74.79 sq. km that affects the physicality of the forest. The impact of salinity is a significant factor in determining the distribution of species and productivity of the mangrove forest of the Sundarbans considerably. Terry Thomas who considered that tidal rise changes vegetative composition and its distribution also vindicates this; and tree growth is noticed to be regulated by the tidal level. It is observed that with the increasing pattern of salinity level in the Bangladeshi Sundarbans from east to west, the density of vegetation growth, its height and canopy decreases from east to west. Moreover, with an increase in salinity level, a significant decrease in regeneration and growth is also observed, which indicates that germination is linked to salinity.

As a corollary of salinity ingression in the Sundarbans, the most of the moderately saline area will transform into strong saline area and the possibility is that less freshwater areas would decline to a large extent along the lower-Baleshwar river in the eastern part of the forest. Due to the constant intrusion of salinity deeper into the Sundarbans, there is a possibility that one type of area with different level of salinity pattern and plant species would be replaced by another level of salinity and species. For instance, Sundari tree, which grows in a fresh water area could be replaced by Gewa; and Gewa could be replaced by the less valuable Goran. With the combined disappearance of both freshwater and moderately saline water area, the Sundarbans would lose over 50% of its merchantable wood. Haq argued that the adverse effects of the burgeoning salinity on the ecosystem of the Sundarbans are manifested in the dying of tops of Sundari trees, retrogression of forest types, slow forest growth, and declined productivity of the forest sites.

The Sundarbans is endowed with a plethora of natural resources, which provides livelihood and opportunities to the inhabitants dependent on it. People in the Sundarbans are mainly engaged in collection of fish, fuel wood, Golpata, crabs, honey and waxes. However, after the agriculture, fisheries are the dominant productive activity providing employment to a large section of the people in this region. Another resource dependent livelihood is honey collection by Mawalis and Golpata collection by the Bawalis, which is also very famous in this region that has been very challenging given the inhospitable and inaccessible forest inside the Sundarbans. The constant decline in the forest cover is posing threat on the livelihood patterns of the people of the Sundarbans. This conspicuous situation has enhanced the conflict between resource and livelihood exacerbated by the displacement and livelihood deprivation. The advent of climate change has augmented the speculations that livelihood such as Mowals, Bawals and Fisher-folks would be worst affected, whereas agriculture is already facing the fury of climate change. The changing patterns of salinity across the Sundarbans have become a curse for agriculture especially during the dry season. Salinity intrusion on the land destroys the soil fertility and agricultural productivity.

It is reported that the natural environment of the Sundarbans is getting hampered due to the salinity and the rise of the water level. As a result, tigers migrate to the zone of fresh water. Specialists assume that most of the tigers of the Indian Sundarbans have moved towards the Bangladeshi portion. Now, it became apparent from the above stated findings that the climate change impact including salinity ingression inside the Sundarbans has caused massive upheaval in the Sundarbans' territory that challenges the orthodox practices of the Sundarbans' management and that is visible in the constant failure of embankments, built to prevent the seawater intruding the islands.

There is growing possibilities that climate change impact will cause serious cross-border security threats between India and Bangladesh.

Huge influx of migration can be seen across the border. These migrations are rampant and are transpiring into the Indian border from the Bangladeshi side, which seem to create burden on Indian resources and raising the fear of conflict among the local population and migrants. It is expected that many millions of Bangladeshi would cross over to India in future owing to the rises in sea level that might further aggravate the ongoing dispute between India and Bangladesh. Huge environmental crisis and the mounting climate change impacts in Bangladesh have triggered cross-border migration to the Indian Sundarban Region. There is a perpetual exodus of migrants from Bangladesh into this region, who could be labeled 'crisis migrants', encroaching into Indian Sundarbans in an anticipation of fears in their own country. Therefore, these people are unnecessarily enmeshed in the orthodox discourse on security and territorial sovereignty between India and Bangladesh. Thus, the blame game begins.

India-Bangladesh relation in the past has witnessed many vicissitudes sometimes leading to friction in their relations. On the other hand, these two countries have also shown an extraordinary cooperation and understanding on many issues of bilateral interest. India and Bangladesh have been characterised and distracted by numerous issues like illegal migration, water sharing, fundamentalism, and Bangladeshi fear of Indian hegemony, the issues generated in wake of the climate change have added a new dimension in the relationship, particularly over the issues of Sundarbans. Any change and damage in one part of the Sundarbans will affect the other part.

Bibliography
(* Indicates a primary source)

A.B. Choudhury, and A. Choudhury (1994), *Mangroves of the Sunderbans*, Vol.1, India, IUCN, Bangkok.

Ahmed, Kazimuddin (2015), "Sunderbans oil spill: who will clean the mess?", [Online: web] Accessed 10 February 2015 URL: http://www.downtoearth.org.in/content/sundarbans-oil-spill-who-will-clean-mess#.VLfv1HPxLqB.

Akhter, Tahera (2009), "Climate Change and Flow of Environmental Displacement in Bangladesh", *UnnayanOnneshan: The Innovators*. pp.1-15.

Akumu, et al. (2011), "Examining the Potential impacts of sea level rise on Coastal wetlands in north-eastern NSW (Australia), *Journal of Coastal Conservation*, Vol.15, No.1, p-15-22

Alam, M. (2003), "Bangladesh Country case study", National Adaptation Programme of Action (NAPA) Workshop, Bhutan, pp.9-11.

Anam, Tahmima (2007), "How Bangladeshis see India", *The Guardian*, 14 August 2007, [Online :web] Accessed 12 March 2015 URL: http://www.theguardian.com/world/2007/aug/14/india.features115.

Arrhenius, S. (1896), "On the influence of carbonic acid in the air upon the temperature of the ground", *Philosophical Magazine*, 41, p.237-276.

Asian Development Bank (2014), *"Climate Action South Asia: Steering Economics Towards low Carbon and Climate resilient development"* CASA Information Update, No.5.

Alam, Sarfaraz (2003), "Environmentally Induced Migration from Bangladesh to India", *Strategic Analysis*, Vol.27, No.3.

Alison et al. (2003), "Stratigraphic evolution of the late Holocene Ganges-Brahmputra lower delta planning sedimentary", *Sedimentary Geology*, 155 (3-4):317-342.

Amin, Muhammad Nurul and Niaz Ahmed Khan (2001), "A Primer on the Nature and Management of the Sunderbans", *Grassroots Voice: A Journal OF Indigenous Knowledge and Development*, Vol.VI, issue: 1, pp.85-101

Banerjee, Bidisha (2010), "The Great Wall of India", *Slate*, 20 December 2010. [Online: web] Accessed 12 March 2015 URL: http://www.slate.com/articles/health_and_science/green_room/2010/12/the_great_wall_of_india.html.

Bast, Joseph L. (2010), *"Seven Theories of Climate change"*, Chicago: The Heartland Institute.

Baylish, John, et al (2008), *The Globalization of World Politics*, and New York: Oxford University Press.

Belt, Don (2011), "The coming Storm", *The National Geographic*, May 2011.

Bhattacharjee, Tapaleena T. et al. (2011), "The Sinking "Beauty"- Sunderbans", *Geospatial World Forum*.

Bhattacharya, A. and Michael Werz (2012), "Climate Change, Migration, and Conflict in South Asia: Rising Tensions and Policy Options Across the Subcontinent", *Center for American Studies*, 3 December 2012, [Online: web] Accessed 5 June 2015 URL:https://www.americanprogress.org/issues/security/report/2012/12/03/46382/climate-change-migration-and-conflict-in-south-asia/.

Biswas, S.R. et al. (2007), "Do invasive plants threaten the Sunderbans mangrove forest of Bangladesh?" *Forest Ecology and Management*, 245:1-9.

Black, Richard (2001), *"Environmental Refugees: Myth or Reality?"* Working Paper No 34, New Issues in Refugee Research, UNHCR, ISSN 1020-7473.

Blasco, F. (1975), *The Mangroves in India* (translated by Mrs. K.Thanikaimoni from LES MANGROVES DE L'INDE), Institute Francais de Pondichery, Inde, Sri Aurobinda Abraham, Pondicherry, India.

Blasco, F. et al. (2001), "Depletion of the mangroves of Continental Asia", *Wetlands Ecology and Management*, 9:245-256.

Bose, Sahana (2009), "Role of Indian Sunderban Mangroves in mitigating climate impacts: An Appraisal", *IOP Science*: 1-2. Retrieved on 26/07/2014

Bose, Sahana (2014), "Illegal migration in the Indian Sunderbans", *Crisis*, FMR 45.

Bose, Sahana, "Human Influence on Mangrove Ecosystem in Indian Sunderbans: An Earth Atmospheric Interaction".

Brown, Oli (2007), "Climate change and forced migration: Observations, projections and implications", Occasional paper for the Human Development Report 2007/2008.

Burroughs, William James (2001), *Climate Change: A Multidisciplinary Approach*, UK: Cambridge University Press.

Center for Science and Environment (2012), *"Living with changing climate: Impact, vulnerability and adaptation challenges in Indian Sundarbans".*

Chanda, S. and Mukherjee, B.B. (1969), "Radio Carbon Dating of Two Microfosiliferous Quaternary Deposites in and around Calcutta, *Sci. & Cult.*, 35: 275-6.

Chandra, Ganesh and R.L.Sagar, "Fisheries in Sunderbans: Problems and Prospects", [Online: web] Accessed 24th January 2015 URL: http://ssrn.com/abstract=2084014.

Chattopadhyay, G.N. et al. (1983), A note on the Possibilities of Salinization of soils under Paddy-cum-brackishwater Aquaculture in Coastal Saline Soils, *J. Indian Soc.Coastal agric. Res.*, 1(1):43-45.

Chen, Junyong (1997), "The Impact of Sea Level Rise on China's Coastal Areas and Its Disaster Hazard Evaluation", *Journal of Coastal Research*, Vo.13, No.3, (Summer, 1997), p.925-30.

Chinnamai, A. Mariyappan, and M. Selvaraj (2011), "Mitigating Climate change: the Indian Perspective", *The Research Journal of Sherubtse College*, p.11-15.

Choudhary, Dr.Navendu (2011), "The Sinking "Beauty"-Sunderbans", *Geospatial World Forum.*

Choudhuri, Sourabh, "Defining Non-traditional Security threats", *Global India Foundation*, [Online: web] Accessed 12 July 2015 URL: http://www.globalindiafoundation.org/nontraditionalsecurity.html.

Choudhury, Biswajit Roy and Pradeep Vyas (2005), *"The Sunderbans"*, New Delhi: RupaPubication India Pvt.Ltd.

Choudhury, J.K. (1997), *Sustainable management of coastal mangrove*, Forest development and social needs, XI World Forestry Congress, Antalya, Turkey.

Chouhan, Chetan (2010), "India, Bangladesh join hands for Sunderbans", *Hindustan Times*, New Delhi, 28 March 2010.

Chowdhury, A.M. (1968), *Working plan of the Sunderban forest Division for the period from 1960-61 to 1979-80*, Vol. I, Government of East Pakistan, Forest Department, Dacca: 82.

Chowdhury, Junayed Ahmed (2012), "Public Participation in Bangladesh's Response to Climate Change Issues", *Advocates for International Development*.

Christensen, B. (1984), *Ecological Aspects of the Sunderbans*, FO: TC P/ BGD/2309 (mf), FAO, Rome, p.42.

Church, J.A. et al. (2013), "Sea Level Change", in Stocker,T.F. et al. (eds.) *Climate Change 2013: The Physical Science Basis*. Contribution of Working Group I to the Fifth Assessment Report of the Intergovernmental Panel on Climate Change, Cambridge: Cambridge University Press.

"Climate Change Laws of Bangladesh" Sabin Center for Climate Change Law, Columbia Law School, [Online: web] Accessed 1 August 2015 URL: http://web.law.columbia.edu/climate-change/resources/climate-change-laws-world/bangladesh.

"Council conclusions on climate change and security," press release, *Council of the European Union*, 8 December 2009.

Danda, Anamitra Anurag (2007), *"Surviving in the Sundarbans: Threats and Responses"* University of Twente, The Netherlands.

Danda, Anamitra Anurag and GayathriSrikanthan (2011), "Indian Sundarbans Delta: A Vision", *WWF Policy Document India*.

Das, S. and Siddiqi, N.A. (1985), "The mangroves and mangrove forest of Bangladesh", Mangrove SilvicultureDivison, Bulletin No.2, Bangladesh Forest Research Institute, Mangrove plantations of the coastal afforestation project. UNDP Project BGD/85/085, Dhaka, Field document No.2.

Dasgupta, S. et al. (2007), "The impacts of Sea level rise on developing countries: a comparative analysis", World Bank Policy Research Working Papar, No. 4136, *The World Bank,* Washington DC.

De Groot, R.S. et al. (2002), "A typology for the classification, description and Valuation of ecosystem functions, goods and services", *Ecological Economics*, 41: 393-408

Deb, S. C. (1956), "Paleoclimatology and Geophysics of the Ganga Delta", *Geographical Review of Inda*, 28: 11-18.

Deka, Dr. Kaustubh (2014), "Bengali Muslims who migrated to Assam in 1871 are not 'illegal Bangladeshis' *Migration Debate* [Online: web] URL:http://scroll.in/article/748027/unravelling-the-mysteries-of-sleep-how-the-brain-sees-dreams.

Desai, Nitin (2010), "Climate Change: economic and historical perspectives", in The Energy and Resources Institute (eds.) *The Environment Emergency: Exploring solutions for a sustainable future*", New Delhi: TERI Press

Devi, Mahasveta (1987), "Where have the workers' wages Gone? Repair of river Embankments in Sunderbans", *Economic &Poloitical Weekly*, vol.22, No.44:1849-1850.

Dhar, Sujoy (2009*), "Hungry Tides in India's Sunderbans" Aljazeera,* 14th December.

Dipanjan Ghosh and Sreeparna Ghosh (2013), "Sunderban Mangroves: Challenges to Survival", *Feature Article*: 44-48.

Douben, K.J. (2006), "Characteristic of river floods and flooding: A global overview, 1985-2003", *Irrigation and Drainage*, 55 (S1), S9-S21.

Dubey, Sourav Kumar (2012), "Climate Change in Sunderban and Adaption Strategy for Aquaculture", access on 27/07/2014 from http://www.academia.edu/3109327/climate_change_ins..

Eckels, H. J. (2008), "Climate change refugees forced to leave Carteret Islands", *Digital Journal.* [Online: web] Accessed 7 March 2015 URL: http://www.digitaljournal.com/article/248946.

El-Raey, M. et al. (1995), "Potential Impacts of Accelerated Sea Level Rise on Alexandaria Governorate, Egypt", *Journal of Coastal Research*, Special Issue No.14, Potentials Impacts of Accelerated Sea Level Rise on Developing Countries" (Spring 1995), p.190-204.

Esty, Daniel C (1999), "Pivotal States and the Environment" in Robert Chase, Emily Hill and Paul Kennedy (eds.) *The Pivotal States: A New Framework for US Policy in the Developing World*, New York: W.W.Nortan and Company p.298-299.

Etkin, David and Elise Ho (2007), "Climate Change: Perceptions and Discourses of Risks", *Journal of Risk Research*, Vol.10, No.5, p.623-624.

Ferguson, H. L. (2008), Twentieth Anniversary of the Toronto Conference on our changing Atmosphere: Implications for Global Security, *Canadian Meteorological and Oceanographic Society (CMOS) Bulletin SCMO*, Vol.36, No.5, p.159.

Few, Roger and FraziskaMatthies (2006), "Flood Hazards and Health: Responding to Present and future Risks", *Earthscan,* London.

Finus, Michael (2002), "Game Theory and International Environemental Cooperation: Any Practical Application?" in Christoph Bohringer, Michael Finus and Carsten Vogt (eds.) *Controlling Global Warming,* Cheltenham, UK: Edward Elgar Publishing Limited.

Fokemma, Syta (2011), *"To be or not to be a climate change refugee, that is the question: An interpretive policy analysis of labeling and framing processes of climate change refugee in Bangladesh"*, Utrecht University.

Friedman, L. (2009*),* "How will climate refugees impact national security? The border between Bangladesh and India may offer a preview of how climate change could destabilize national", [Online: web] Accessed 7 March 2015 URL: http://www.scientificamerican.com/article/climage-refugees-national-security/.

"Global warming 'biggest threat'," BBC News, 9 January 2004.

Gain, Philip (1998), *"Bangladesh Land Forest and Forest People"*, Dhaka: Society for Environment and Human Development (SEHD).

Gain, Philip (2002), *"Bangladesh Environment Facing the 21st Century"*, Dhaka: Society for Environment and Human Development (SEHD).

Gain, Philip (2002), *"The Last Forests of Bangladesh"*, Dhaka: Society for Environment and Human Development (SEHD).

Ghosh, A.K. (1941), "Submerged Forests in Calcutta", Sci. & Cult., 6: 669-70.

Ghosh, Arun (Feb 20, 1988), "The Sunderbans", *Economic & Political Weekly*, vol.23, No.8:352-356.

Ghosh, Debabrata (2009), "The Hungry Tide: Rise in Sea Levels in the Sundarbans Due to Global Warming-Induced Climate Change", *International Journal of South Asian Studies*, pp.342-352.

Glick P, et al. (2008), "Sea level rise and Coastal Habitats in the Chesapeake Bay Region, Technical Report", *National Wildlife Federation,* USA.

"Golpata collection goes on in Sunderbans" (2012) [online:web] Accessed 24th January 2015 URL:http://www.thefinancialexpressbd.com/old/index.php?ref=MjBfMTJfMThfMTJfMV85MV8xNTM0NjE=.

Gopinath, G. and P Seralathan (2005), "Rapid coastal erosion of the Sagar Island, West Bengal", *Environmental Geology*, Springer Berlin Heidelberg. Vol. 48 No. 8, p. 1058-1067.

*"Greenhouse Effect and its Impact on the Region" a joint study undertaken under the declaration of the Fourth SAARC Summit (Islamabad, 29-31 December 1988) to provide a basis for a meaningful cooperation among member states, which completed in 1992, [Online: web] URL: http://www.saarc-sec.org/userfiles/Large%20Publications/RSGEIOR/index.php.

Gupta, Smita (2015), "Parliament puts seal of approval on LBA", *The Hindu*, Delhi, 8 May 2015.

Gupta, Subhadip and Gargi Sarkar (2014), "Climate Change and Economic Adaptability of Indian Sunderban", *Journal of Economic and Sustainable Development*, Vol.5, No. 22.

Halden, Peter (2007), "The Geopolitics of Climate change: Challenges to the International System", *FOI, Swedish Defence Research Agency*, Stockholm, Sweden.

Haq, Syed Azizul (2010), "Impact of climate change on Sunderbans", a paper presented in 18th Commonwealth Forestry Conference 2010 on 28 June-02 July 2010 at Edinburg International Conference Center, Scotland, UK.

Hartmann, D.L. et al (2013), "Observations: Atmosphere and Surface", in Stocker, T.F., D. Qin, G.-K. Plattner, M. Tignor, S.K. Allen, J. Boschung, A. Nauels, Y. Xia, V. Bex and P.M. Midgley (eds.) *Climate Change 2013: The Physical Science Basis. Contribution of Working Group I to the Fifth Assessment Report of the Intergovernmental Panel on Climate,* Cambridge: Cambridge University Press,

Hazra et al. (2002), "Sea Level and associated changes in the Sunderbans", *Science and Culture,* vol.68, no 9-12, p.309-321.

Hazra, S. and Bakshi, A. (2003), *Environmental Refugees from Vanishing Islands. Environment and Human Security,* India: Lancers Books Publications, pp. 219-227.

Hazra, S. et al. (2010), 'Temporal Change Detection (2001-2008) Study of Sundarban', *School of Oceanographic Studies*, Jadavpur University, Kolkata.

HazraSugata, "Climate Change Policy paper II: Climate Change Adaptation in Coastal Region of West Bengal".

Heining, R.L. (1892), *Working plan of Sunderbans government forest,* Khulna and 24-Parganas district, Bengal, Calcutta, Bengal Secretariat Press.

Hemming, D. et al. (2007), *"Impacts of Mean Sea Level Rise Based on current state of the Art Modelling"*, Hadley Centre for Climate Prediction and Research, Exeter, UK.

Homer-Dixon, Thomas (1994): "Environmental Scarcities and Violent Conflict: Evidence from Cases", *International Security*, 19(1): 5-40.

Hussain, D. (2009), "Fencing off Bangladesh: India's 2500-mile border fence is meant to keep out smugglers, but simply living on the boundary is a dangerous business", [Online: web] Accessed 7 March 2015 URL: http://www.theguardian.com/commentisfree/2009/sep/05/bangladesh-india-border-fence.

Hussain, Mohammad Asad et al. (2013), "Changes of the Seasonal Salinity Distribution at the Sundarbans Coast due to Impact of climate change", 4th International Conference on Water & Flood Management (ICWFM-2013), P.637-648.

India-Bangladesh Sunderbans Ecosystem Forum to be launched [Online: web] URL: http://www.thehindu.com/todays-paper/indiabangladesh-sunderbans-ecosystem-forum-to-be-launched/article744688.ece

*IPCC (2001), "Climate Change 2001:Impacts, Adaptation and Vulnerability", J. J. McCarthy, O. F. Canziani, N. A. Leary, D. J. Dokken and K. S. White (eds.), Cambridge: Cambridge University Press.

Jogoo, V. (1992), *"Assessing the Impacts-Mauritius Case Study"*, Presented at the International workshop, The Rising challenge of the Sea, Margarita, Venezuela March 1992.

Juneja, Sugandh (2012), "Sunderbans at risk", [Online: web] Accessed 10 March 2015 URL: http://www.downtoearth.org.in/content/sundarbans-risk.

Kaizer, Fahad (2014), "A day with 'Mowals-The hunters of golden liquid", [online:web] Accessed 24th January 2015 URL: http://www.dhakacourier.com.bd/a-day-with-%E2%80%98mawals%E2%80%99-%E2%80%93-the-hunters-of-golden-liquid/.

Kathirensen, K. and Rajendran N. (2005), Grow mangroves for protecting coral reefs, SDMRI Research Publications

Korgan, F.N. (1997), "Global draught watch from space", *Bulletin of the American Meteorological society*, 78, 621-636.

Kumar, Chirantan (2009), "Migration and Refugee issues between India and Bangladesh", *Scholars Voice: A New Way of Thinking*, Vol.1, No.1, pp.64-89.

Kumar, Pushpam (2012), "Impact of economic drivers on mangroves of Indian Sunderbans: an exploration of missing links", *Environ Dev Sustain* 14: 939-953.

Kushol, R. et al. (2009), "Cyclone *Aila, Initial Assessment Report, with focus on Khulna district*" UnnayanOnneshan, Humanity Watch and Nijera Kori, Dhaka.

Lama, Mahendra P. (2008), "Internal displacement in India: causes, protection and dilemmas", *Forced Migration Review,* 8 pp.24-26.

Lama, Mahendra P. (2015), "India and its Neighbours: Policy Priorities for the New Government", a Valedictory address delivered on 25th March 2015 in an International Conference at Centre for South Asian Studies, Jawaharlal Nehru University: New Delhi.

Litchfield, William Alex (2010), "Climate change Induced Extreme weather events & Sea level Rise in Bangladesh leading to Migration and conflict", *ICE Case Studies*:1-18, [Online : web] Accessed 26 July 2014 URL: file:///G:/Untitled Folder/Climate Change Induced Extreme weather...

Lok Sabha Secretariate(2013), "Climate Change- India's Perspective", Members' Reference Service, No. 25 / RN / Ref. / August/ 2013, p.9.

Loucks, Colby et al. (2010), "Sea level rise and tigers: predicted impacts to Bangladesh's Sunderbans mangroves", *Climatic Change*, 98:291-298.

Mackinder, H. J. (1904), "The Geographical Pivot of History." *The Geographical Journal*, 23 (4), 421-442.

*Ministry of Environment and Forest, Government of India (2003), "Working Paper", [Online: web] Accessed 10 July 2015 URL: http://www.moef.nic.in/sites/default/files/nfc-wpaper.pdf.

*Ministry of Environment and Forest, Government of India (2010), Report to the People on Environment and Forest 2009-2010.

*Ministry of Environment& Forests, Government of India, Annual Report 2012-13.

*Ministry of Environment, Forest and Climate Change, Government of India, "Introduction", [Online: web] Accessed on 1 July 2015 URL: http://envfor.nic.in/division/introduction-10.

*Ministry of Environment, Forest and Climate Change, Government of India, "Environment Protection", [Online: web] Accessed 1 July 2015 URL: http://envfor.nic.in/division/environment-protection.

*Ministry of External Affairs, Government of India (2011), "MOU between India and Bangladesh on Conservation of the Sunderban", [Online: web] Accessed 27 May 2015 URL: http://mea.gov.in/bilateraldocuments.htm?dtl/5141/MOU+ between+India+and+ Bangladesh+on+Conservation+of+the+Sundarban.

Mahadevia, Kanksha and MayankVikash, "Climate change-Impact on the Sunderbans: A case Study", *International Scientific Journal Environmental Science,* [Online: web] Accesssed 7 July 2015 URL: http://environment.scientific- journal.com/articles/2/1.pdf.

Mandal, R.N. et al. (2010)," Dwindling Indian Sunderban Mangrove: The Way out", *Science and Culture*, 76(7-8): 275-282.

Mangrove Forests threatened by the climate Change in the Sunderbans of India and Bangladesh", Retrieved on 27/07/2014 from http://climateimc.org/en/originalnews/ 2013/01/16/mangrove-forest.

Maxine van Bommel (2010), *Good fences don't make good neighbours: Outlining the complexities of protecting climate displaces, with special reference to India and Bangladesh"*, Utrecht University.

McGranahan, G. et al. (2007), "The rising tide: assessing the risks of climate change and human settlements in low elevation coastal Zones", *Environment and Urbanization*, Vol.19, No.17, p.17-37.

Md. Jinnahtul Islam, at al. (1997), "Remote Sensing for change detection in the Sunderbans, Bangladesh", *Geocarto International*, 12:3, 91-100.

Menon, Meena (2015), "Tiger Census Good News from The Jungle: Giant leap for big Cat", *The Hindu*, Delhi, 21 January 2015.

Michael A Toman, Ujjayany Chakraborty, Shreekant Gupta (eds.) *India and Global Climate Change: Perspective on Economic and Policy From a Developing Country"*, India: Oxford University Press.

Minar, M.H. et al. (2013), "Climate Change and Coastal Zone of Bangladesh: Vulnerability, Resilience and Adaptability", *Middle-East Journal of Scientific Research*, 13 (1): 114-120.

Mishra, A.K. et al. (2010), "Impact of global warming and climate change on social development", *Journal of Comparative social welfare*, 26:2-3, 239-260.

Mitra, A. et al. (2009), " Observed changes in water mass properties in the Indian Sundarbans (northwestern Bay of Bengal) during 1980–2007", *Current Science*, Vol. 97, No. 10, pp. 1445-1452.

Mitra,A. et al. (2009), "Pulse of climate change in Sunderbans: a myth or reality?" *Natl AcadSci Lett* 32:1-2.

"Mowals Busy for Collecting Honey in Sunderbans", [online:web] Accessed 24th January 2015 URL: https://www.highbeam.com/Registration/Registration1.

Mukherjee, B. B. (1972), "Quaternary Pollen Analysis as a Possible Indicator of PrehistoricAgriculture in the Deltaic Part of West Bengal, *J. Palynol.*, 8: 144-51.

Mukherjee, S. K. (1969), "Survey of Plants Resources of India and its Use", *Bull. Bot. Surv. India*, 11 (3&4): 217-23.

Murthy, Alexander B. and DemianHommel, *"The Geopolitical Implications of Environmental Change"*, University of Oregon, Eugene, Oregon: USA.

Musa, A.R.M.A. (2010), "Latest news on climate displacement in Bangladesh: Displacement Solutions", [Online: web] Accessed 7 March 2015, URL: http://displacementsolutions.org/ latest-news-on-climate-displacement-in-bangladesh/.

*National Communication (NATCOM) (2004), Chapter 3: *"Vulnerability Assessment and Adaptation"*, India's Initial National Communication to the UNFCCC, Ministry of Environment and Forests, Government of India.

"National security and the threat of climate change," military advisory board, Center for Naval Analysis Corporation, 2007.

Nandy, S. and S. Bandyopadhyay (2008), "'Trend of sea level change in the Hugli Estuary, West Bengal", *Souvenir and Abstracts Volume*, 21st Conference of Indian Institute of Geomorphology, Tripura University, pp. 83-84.

Naskar, K. R. and A.P. Sharma (2010). Coastal zone vegetation in India with reference to mangroves and need for their conservation.

Naskar, K.R. (1981), *Floristic Studies of the District 24-Parganas in West Bengal (India) with special Reference to the Mangrove vegetation of the Sunderbans,*Ph.D Thesis, University of Calcutta.

Naskar, K.R. (1983), Halophytes and their Unique Adaptation on the Sunderbans Mangrove Swamps in India, *J. Indian Soc. Coastal agric. Res,* 1(2):91-105.

Naskar, K.R. and GuhaBakshi, D.N. (1982), Sunderbans-the world famous Mangrove forest of the District 24- Parganas in West Bengal, *J.Econ.Tax. Botany*, 3: 883-918.

Naskar, Kumudranjan and D. N. GuhaBakshi (1987), *Mangrove Swamps of the Sundarbans: an Ecological Perspective,* Calcutta: NayaProkash.

Nath, Shloka (2011*), "Environmental Diplomacy: Saving the Sunderbans and Restoring Indo-Bangladesh Friendship"*, Mumbai: Gateway House: Indian Council on Global Relations.

Neves, Claudia F. and Dieter Muche (1995), "Potentials Impacts of Sea Level Rise on the Metropolitan Region of Recife, Brazil", *Journal of Coastal Research*, Special Issue, No. 14, Potential Impacts of Accelerated Sea-Level Rise on Developing countries (Spring 1995), p.116-31.

Nicholls, Robert J. (2004), "Coastal Flooding and Wetland loss in the 21st Century: Changes under the SRES climate and socioeconomic scenarios", *Global Environmental change*, Vo.14, No.1, p.69-86.

Nicholls, Robert J. Et al. (1999), "Increasing flood risk and wetland losses due to global sea-level rise: regional global analyses", Global Environmental Change, Vol. 9, p.69-87.

"Our changing atmosphere: Implications for global security," Secretariat of the World Meteorological Organization, conference proceedings, 27-30 June 1988.

"Obama announces plans to achieve energy independence", *Washington Post*, January 26th 2009. [Online: web] Accessed 12 July 2015 URL:http://www.washingtonpost.com/wp-dyn/content/article/2009/01/26/AR2009012601147_2.html?sid=ST2009012601175.

Pachaury, R.K. (2004), "Global Climate Change: Indian Perspective Revisited and Restated", in Michael A. Toman, Ujjayant Chakraborty, and Shreekant Gupta (eds.) *India and Global Climate Change: Perspective on Economic and Policy From a Developing Country,* India: Oxford University Press. p. 341-346.

Panda, Architesh (2010), "Climate Refugees: Implications for India", *Economic &Political Weekly*, vol.XLV no.20: 76-79.

Pandey, Kundan (2014), "India on high alert after massive oil spill threatens Sunderbans ecology", [Online: web] Accessed 10 February 2015 URL: http://www.downtoearth.org.in/content/india-high-alert-after-massive-oil-spill-threatens-sunderbans-ecology.

Pandey, Kundan (2014), "Oil spill in Bangladesh's Sela river threatens dolphin sanctuary", [Online:web] Accessed 10 February 2015 URL: http://www.downtoearth.org.in/content/oil-spill-bangladesh-s-sela-river-threatens-dolphin-sanctuary.

Parsons, Claudia (2009), *"Small islands win UN vote on climate change security," Reuters*, 3 June 2009, [Online: web] Accessed 12 July 2015 URL: http://www.reuters.com/article/2009/06/03/us-un-security-idUSTRE5525W920090603.

Patil, R.P. (1962), "Our Mangrove Resources", Trop. Ecol.3, ½, 70-1.

Perry, Jim (2011), "World Heritage hot spots: a global model identifies the 16 natural heritage properties on the world Heritage List most at risk from climate change", *International Journal of Heritage Studies,* 17:5, 426-441, DOI: 10.1080/13527258.2011.568064.

Prabhat Kumar Rai and Prashant Kumar Rai. 2013. "Environmental and socio-economic impacts of global climate change: An overview on mitigation approaches", *Environmental Skeptics and Critics*, 2(4): 126-148.

Prabhat Kumar Rai and Prashant Kumar Rai. 2013. "Paradigms of global climate change and sustainable development: Issues and related policies", *Environmental Skeptics and Critics*, 2(2):30-45.

Prakash, A. and Shailja Menon (2011), "Fenced Indians Pay for 'Security'", *Economic & Political Weekly*, Vol.XLVI, No.12, pp.33-37.

Purdy, Margaret $ Leanne Smythe (2010), From Obscurity to action: Why Canada must tackle the security dimensions of climate change, *International Journal Spring.*

Qureshi, I.M. (1959), "Botanical, Silvicultural features of Mangroves forests of Bombay state", *Proc. Mangrove Symposium*, Faridabad, India, pp.20-26.

Ragoonaden, Sachooda (1997), "Impact of Sea Level Rise on Mauritius", *Journal of Coastal Research, Special Issue,* No.24, Island States At Risk: Global Climate Change, Development and Population (Fall 1997), p.205-223.

Raha, Atanu et al. (2012), "Climate Change impacts on Indian Sunderbans: a time series analysis (1924-2008)", *Biodivers Conserve*, 21:1289-1307.

Rahman, M R and M Asaduzzaman (2010), "Ecology of Sunderban, Bangladesh", *J. Sci., Foundation,* 8(1&2): 35-47.

Rajagopal, K. (2014), "SC: why is eastern border still porous?", *The Hindu*, 18 December 2014.

Rajagopal, Krishnadas (2015), "Centre, Assam delaying border fencing: SC", *The Hindu*, Delhi, 14 May 2015.

Rajan, Chella S. (2008), *"Blue Alert",* Greenpeace India

Ramachandran, Smiriti Kak (2015), "Punish politicians shielding illegal immigrants", *The Hindu*, Delhi, 14 May 2015.

Rashid, S. Harun. et al. (2008), "Undergrowth Species diversity of Sunderban mangrove Forest (Bangladesh) in relation to Salinity", *Ber.Inst. Landschefts-PFlanzenokologic Uni. Hohenheim Heft*: 41-56.

Ray, Dr. Tapan (2013), "Traditional Honey Collecting: Emerging Livelihoods Problems And Socio-economic uplift of Mawalis Community in Sunderbans", Department of Bengali, Karimganj College, Karimganj, Assam, India, Vol.II, Issue II.

Renner, M. (2005), "Security redefined", in L. Stark (eds.) *State of the World 2005: redefining global security.* Worldwatch Institute, p. 3-19.

Salinity threatens the world Heritage "The Sunderban of Bangladesh"- Published by PRDI-*Participatory Research and Development Initiative.*

Sarkar, Khalekuzzaman (2013), "Fisher Livelihoods in the Sunderbans". [Online: web] URL: ewcbookstore.org/fox/foxRuralLivelihoods 005-ch04.pdf (2014).

Sarker, Sonia (2011), "Running with the wolves", The Telegraph, India, 24 July 2011, [Online: Web] Accessed 10 March 2015 URL: http://www.telegraphindia.com/1110724/jsp/7days/story_14280419.jsp.

Sen, Malcolm (2009), "Spatial Justice: The Ecological imperative and Post colonial development", *Journal of Post Colonial Writing*, 45:4,365-377, DOI: 10.1080/17449850903273507.

Sen, P. and M. Banerjee (1984), "On the occurrence of Reptilian Remmants in the Peat Bed of Barrackpore, 24-Parganas, West Bengal, *Paleobot. Soc. Ind.*, 29: 47-51.

Sengupta, Debjani (2011), "From Dandakaranya to Marichjhapi: rehabilitation, representation and the partition of Bengal (1947)", *Social Semiotics*, 21:1, 101-123, DOI: 10.1080/10350330.2011.535673.

Sengupta, Samrat and Dr. Prakash Rao (2003), "Adverse Impacts of Climate Change: Perception and Responses of Local community", UNFCCC Expert Workshop on Local coping strategies for Adaptation, 12-13 November 2003, New Delhi.

Shah, Sudhir A. (2004), "A Noncooperative Theory of Emissions –Cap Determination", in Michael A. Toman, Ujjayant Chakraborty, Shreekant Gupta (eds.) *India and Global Climate Change: Perspective from a developing Country,* India: Oxford University Press.

Singh, O. P. (2007), 'Spatial variation of sea level trend along the Bangladesh coast', *Mar Geol*, 25: 205-212.

Singh, O.P. (2002), "Spatial variation of sea level trend along the Bangladesh coast", *Mar Geol*, 25: 205-212.

Singh, O.P. (2007), "Long-term trends in the Frequency of severe cyclones of Bay of Bengal: Observations and simulations", *Mausam*, 58(16), pp.59-66.

Singh, Shiv Sahay (2015), "Report underestimates tiger count in Sunderbans", *The Hindu*, Delhi, 23 January 2015.

Sinha Ray, S.P. (2010), "Status of Ground water condition in Sunderbans area, West Bengal Commissioned Report.

Sinha, S.K. (1998). *Illegal migration into Assam, a report submitted to the president of India.*

Sivakumar, Mannava V.K. and Robert Stefanski, "Climate change in South Asia" Chapter 2, [Online: web] Accessed 17 July 2015 URL: file:///C:/Users/Prashant%20Kr.%20Sharma/Downloads/9789048195152-c2.pdf.

Sharma, Prashant Kumar (2017), "Climate Change: Tracing the Inception of its Scientific and Political Discourse", *Mainstream Weekly*, Vol LV No. 22, New Delhi, 20 May 2017, ISSN: 0542-1462/RNI No.: 7064/62.

Sharma, Prashant Kumar (2017), "Assessing Vicissitudes in India-Bangladesh Relations: An Environmental Perspective", *South Asia Democratic Forum (SADF)*, Issue No. 89, 1June 2017: Brussels, ISSN: 2406-5617.

Smith, Anthony Oliver (2009), "Sea Level Rise and the Vulnerability of Coastal Peoples: Responding to the Local Challenges of Global Climate Change in the 21st Century", *United Nations University-UNU-EHS-Institute for Environment and Human Security*, No.7/2009:1-52.

Sohela, Mustari (2013), "The Challenges and Coping Strategies of 'Mowal' the Honey collectors of Sunderban, Bangladesh", *International Research Journal of Social Sciences*, vol.2 (6) 7-11.

Spasov, MA Nikolco. "Global Geopolitical Implications for the World As A Result of the Negative Impacts of Climate Change", *Scientific Article*, 551.583 (100).

Special Correspondent (2014), "6 lakh working people in Sunderbans need hospital", [online: web] Accessed 24th January 2015 URL: http://thedailynewnation.com/news/8090/6-lakh-working-people-in-sundarbans-need-hospital.html.

Special correspondent (2014), "Development 'threatens fragile Sunderbans'in Bangladesh", *The Hindu*, Delhi, 20 December 2014.

Spykman, N.J. (1944), "*The Geography of the Peace*", New York: Harcourt, Brace and Campany.

Swain, Ashok (1996), "Displacing the Conflict: Environmental Destruction in Bangladesh and Ethnic Conflicts in India", *Journal of Peace Research*, Vol.33, No.2, pp.189-204.

"Strategic trends programme: Future character of conflict," February 2010; and *"Adaptability and partnership: Issues for the strategic defence review,"* green paper presented to parliament by the minister of state for defence, United Kingdom, February 2010.

"Sunderban is Sick: 40% Forest Affected by Top-Dying", *Earth Touch*, No.3/ February 1997.

Terri (2010), "*Environment Emergency*", New Delhi: The Energy and Resource Institute.

*The World Bank (2014), *Building Resilience for Sustainable Development of the Sundarbans: Strategy Report*, JS Print O Pack: New Delhi.

"*The first national security statement to the Australian parliament,*" address by the prime minister of Australia, December 4th 2008.

"The Great Sunderbans (Bangladesh and India): Forest swamp, draw only border, UNESCO World Heritage Site', [Online: web] Accessed 24th January 2015 URL: http://wikimapia.org/1651148/The-Great-Sundarbans-Bangladesh-and-India.

"Tigers Kills wood collector" (2011) [online:web] Accessed 24th January 2015 URL:http://bdnews24.com/details.php?id=183227&cid=2.

"Traditional and Non-traditional Security," *Institute for Security & Development Policy*, [Online: web] Accessed 12 July 2015 URL: http://www.isdp.eu/issues/traditional-and-non-traditional-security.html.

The India- Bangladesh Sundarbans Ecosystem Forum to be launched in September [Online: web] URL: http://www.ecosensorium.org/2010/04/india-bangladesh-sundarbans-ecosystem.html.

Tomlinson, P.B. (1986), *The Botany of Mangrove*, Cambridge: Cambridge University Press.

Trimble, P.J. (1998), "Preliminary Estimate of Impacts of Sea-Level Rise on the Regional Water Resources of Southern Florida", *Journal of Coastal Research*, Special Issue, No.26. Proceedings of the Palm Beach International Coastal Symposium, 19-23 May (Spring 1998), p.252-55.

Uddin, M.S. (2011*), Economic Valuation of Sunderbans mangrove ecosystem services- A case study in Bangladesh*, M.Sc. thesis, UNESCO-IHE, Netherlands.

Uddin,Md. Shams, et al. (2013), "Climate Change on the Sunderbans Mangrove ecosystem services and dependent livelihoods in Bangladesh", *Asian Journal of Conservation Biology,* Vol.2, N. 2: 152-156.

United Nations Security Council (2007), "Security Council holds first-ever debate on impact of climate change on Peace, Security, hearing over 50 speakers", [Online: web] Accessed 12 July 2015 URL: http://www.un.org/press/en/2007/sc9000.doc.htm.

Unnikrishnan, A.S. et al (2006), 'Sea level changes along the Indian coast: observations and projections', *Current Science*, Vol. 90 No. 3, pp. 362-368.

URL:http://www.preventionweb.net/files/8203_SalinityandMangrove.pdf.

Vishnu Mitre and H.P. Gupta (1972), "Pollen Analysis Study of Quaternary Deposits in the Bengal Basin", *Paleobotanist,* 19: 297-306.

Walker, Jamie and Andrew Faulkner (2007), "Keelty warning on global warming," *The Australian*, 25 September 2007, [Online: web] Accessed 12 July 2015 URL: http://www.theaustralian.com.au/archive/news/keelty-warning-on-global-warming/story-e6frg8gf-1111114495562.

Warrick, R.A. and Oerlemans, J. (1990).Sea level rise. In 'Climate Change: The IPCC Scientific Assessment', Houghton, J.T., Jenkins, G.J. and Ephraums, J.J. (Ed.), Cambridge University Press, p. 257-281.

Wilhite, D.A. (2000), "Draught as a natural hazard: Concepts and definitions", in D.A. Wilhite (eds) *Draught: A global assessment*, p.3-18, Natural Hazards and Disasters series, London: Routledge Publishers.

WWF Report India (2010), "Sundarbans: Future Imperfect: Climate Adaptation Report".

Yadav, J.S.P. et al. (1979), "Coastal Saline Soils of India", *CSSRI Bull,* No.5, pp.6-34.

Yadav, J.S.P. et al. (1981), "Management of coastal Saline Soils of Sunderbans", *Bull 7 (CSSRI-ICAR),* Karnal, India, pp.1-32.

Zahan, Nushrat (2008), "Environmental Security: Coping with climate security of Bangladesh", *Issue Brief, Bangladesh Institute of Peace and Security Studies*, Issue 3, pp.1-8.

Index